The Beginning Writer's Answer Book

The Beginning Writer's Answer Book

Revised Edition

Edited by
Kirk Polking, Jean Chimsky
and Rose Adkins

Writer's Digest Books
Cincinnati, Ohio

Library of Congress Catalog Card Number 78-102028
ISBN 0-911654-50-X

Contents

Contents

1. Definitions of Writing Terms ....

If an editor calls your writing "pedestrian," you'd bette
know what he means. The writer's world is filled witl
terms and abbreviations—SASE, query, potboiler, ki
fee, think piece—that can sometimes confuse even th
most seasoned pro.

2. Education for Writers ....

A writer's education doesn't begin and end behind th
typewriter. He should investigate college and correspond
ence courses, fellowships, grants, and other educationa
pursuits to help him become a more well-rounded writer.

3. Getting Started in Freelancing ....

It takes more than raw talent to break into print. Othe
prerequisites are a thorough knowledge of the market
strict adherence to submission requirements, a clear
manuscript, and a pinch of luck.

4. Preparing the Manuscript ....

No need to count every word in that story before you

send it to *Redbook*; there's a formula you can use that will estimate the number of words for you. Know the mechanics of manuscript preparation and you'll increase your sales.

Digging for facts requires knowledge of available resources and the persistence to keep looking until you find that piece of information you need. The writer must know how to organize his data, credit sources, and get permission to reprint.

When an editor says, "Query first," the writer had better load plenty of ammo into his letter if he wants a go-ahead. He should also know what to include in the query and how long to wait for a response.

The line between fair and unfair use of copyrighted material is as thin as a sheet of typing paper. Any writer who plans to use material that came from the lips—or the typewriter—of another person should be familiar with fair use guidelines and procedures.

How should the writer handle anecdotes? Is it possible to make simultaneous submissions? What should the writer do when a magazine publishes his work, but doesn't pay for it? You'll find answers in this chapter.

Though newspapers usually don't pay as much as magazines for their material, they are still a big market for the freelance writer. You'll find tips on newspaper freelancing and how to get a position on the staff of a newspaper included in this chapter.

Approaching a complete stranger for an interview can be a nerve-shattering experience. To soothe your nerves, you'll find advice in this chapter on getting the interview, tape recorder etiquette, and contacting celebrities.

Pictures are not always worth a thousand words, but they can sometimes help sell a thousand words, so you should know how to obtain photos from stock photo agencies, buy a camera, use a model release, and copyright a photo.

Whether you are writing a novel or a short-short story, you should know how to create conflict and believable characters. In this chapter, you'll also find advice on finding the right market for your story and how to fictionalize fact.

Reading your eyes out will help you get a firm grasp of the styles of various writers. Don't try to imitate these writers, though; give yourself a free hand to develop your own personal style.

Each type of market—religious, trade journal, confession, general-interest—has peculiarities of which the writer should be aware. Knowing these taboos before you submit will greatly increase your chances of acceptance.

wind up enemies if they're not careful. Get the specific
of your arrangement down on paper at the beginning o
your relationship and you'll avoid squabbles in th
future.

Think you need an agent to sell your work? Most agent
will only work with established writers, while those who
will look at the work of beginners usually charge a read
ing fee. You should be aware of what the agent can do
for you, what qualities to look for in an agent, and
where to find their names and addresses.

Few poets are able to make a living from their work, bu
that doesn't mean they aren't dedicated. Read this chap
ter for hints on preparing the poem for submission and
publishing poetry collections.

Got a tune going 'round and 'round inside your head
Song writing and marketing is a tough business, but no
impossible to break into. Before you begin, you should
know how to cut a "demo," copyright a song, and find
names and addresses of music publishers.

Sending a manuscript from your home to the editor'
desk can be an expensive, frustrating experience. Writer
should know the difference between certified mail and
registered mail and they should also know how to us
the special fourth class manuscript rate.

Rejection slips are the bane of the writer's existence. Writers should know when to give up on a repeatedly rejected manuscript and what the editor means when he says a manuscript "needs more punch."

terial you should submit to a syndicate, and how to self-syndicate your work.

In this chapter, you'll find out how to track down that famous/infamous author to tell him how much you liked/hated his most recent work.

Knowing the tricks of the trade is one of the tricks of the trade of successful writing. Authors should know how to obtain sample copies of a magazine, the correct way to query a chain publisher, and how the publisher evaluates manuscripts.

Translations present special problems. Writers should know how to request permission to translate and reprint and how to find markets for translations.

Every writer should know where research ends and plagiarism begins, and under what circumstances he needs permission to use a quote. Writers should also know how to determine how much is fair use.

Specialized materials—epigrams, children's books, proverbs, comedy skits, comic books—present unique problems. In this chapter, the writer will find advice on how to handle the writing and marketing of his specialized work.

Preface

Question: What are first North American serial rights?

Question: Can I copyright my article before it is published?

Question: Should a manuscript be single-spaced or double-spaced?

Question: Is it best to query a book publisher before sending the completed manuscript?

If you don't know the answers to the above questions, you need *The Beginning Writer's Answer Book.* But don't let the title fool you, for within these pages lie answers even the seasoned pro will appreciate. Included in this completely revised edition are questions writers most often ask the editors of WRITER'S DIGEST arranged under subject categories for the reader's convenience in quickly locating an answer.

Here you will find discussions on trends in the marketplace (including taboos); the new copyright law and what it means to the writer; writing for TV; "rights" bought by magazines; finding photos to illustrate the nonfiction manuscript; interpreting rejections; fair use standards in reprinting copyrighted material; using a pen name, and more.

For additional information on these subjects, the writer is referred to books and reference volumes that can supply a more in-depth answer to his specific question. Other publications that keep popping up in answers are WRITER'S MARKET and WRITER'S DIGEST magazine, both of which contain comprehensive market information as well as professional advice for writers. WRITER'S DIGEST has been indexed in the *Readers' Guide to Periodical Literature* from January 1968 through, December 1977; and in *Access: The Supplementary Index to Periodicals* from January 1978 to present.

A word of warning: Information presented herein is meant to serve as a general guideline only and is not intended to substitute for legal advice. If you have a question about a specific clause in your book contract or some other point of law, consult an attorney.

If you have a writing-related question, or a suggestion for the next revision of this book, by all means drop the editors a note. If you want a reply, though, be sure to enclose SASE.

What's an SASE?

You'll find the answer in the first chapter.

The Editors

1. Definitions of Writing Terms

SASE

Q. *What does SASE mean? And why is SASE in almost every market listing in* WRITER'S DIGEST *and* WRITER'S MARKET?

A. SASE means self-addressed, stamped envelope. It is to be enclosed in every query, every manuscript submission, to every market editor. When requesting information from an editor or from a magazine's subscription or service departments, it's always best to enclose SASE to cover return postage and reply from that market. Make sure the envelope is a #10 envelope at least—nothing like the tiny personal-size stationery envelopes, which are useless when sending reprints of articles, flyers on publications, or literature which is requested. And when submitting a manuscript, always enclose the proper size envelope (usually the same size as the one the manuscript was mailed in), with correct postage for return. Remember: some editors will not return material that is submitted without SASE.

Market

Q. *What is meant by a "market"—and what does the phrase "marketing your material" mean? I've often seen both referred to in* WRITER'S DIGEST.

A. A "market" is a magazine, publishing firm, or company to which you sell what you write. "Marketing your material" means selling what you write. "Study the market" means just that—study the magazine or book firm's editorial requirements in the market listings in writers' publications, so you will understand what type of material the market is purchasing. Also, study the market itself—read back issues of the magazine, or in the case of a book publisher, study the company's catalog.

Little Magazines

Q. *Beginning writers are usually advised to try to sell their writing to "little magazines" rather than bigger and better known ones. My problem is this: Which ones are the "little magazines" and where may I obtain a list of them?*

A. There is a difference between "little magazines" and "lesser known" magazines. This distinction has to do with the fact that in literary circles, the term "little magazines" refers primarily to those publications frequently published by universities, which, though often nonpaying, do print works of high literary caliber and social consciousness. "Lesser known" magazines are those which do not pay as much as the top slicks, for example, but do use similar material. "Little" and "lesser known" publications offer the writer a vehicle for expression that often can't be found in the commercial press. The drawbacks are little or no pay and often an excessive amount of time taken to report on and return submissions. Lists of these publications, their submission requirements, payment scales and preferred subject matter may be found in the Literary and "Little" Publications and Alternative Publications sections of WRITER'S MARKET. Other lesser known publications are scattered throughout WRITER'S MARKET, in various categories.

Query?

Q. *I am a newcomer to the wonderful world of writing and I am constantly confronted with the word: query. Is there a special or preferred form for a query? What is a query?*

A. The query is a letter to an editor attempting to sell him on the idea of your article or book. It can be as short as a couple paragraphs on one page or it could be two or three pages single-spaced, depending on the particular market and the complexity of the subject. Writers submitting article ideas to magazines are encouraged to limit their queries to no more than one page.

Subheads

Q. *What do editors call the small descriptive sentence that usually appears under the main title of an article?*

A. Most editors call it a "subhead." A subhead is usually designed to pique the reader's interest in reading the article or story by telling just a little bit about the subject matter.

Collectibles

Q. *I've seen the word "collectibles" in some of the market listings in* Writer's Digest. *What does "collectibles" mean?*

A. Collectibles can refer to magazines that cater to antiques and collecting of same. More often, the word "collectible" refers to the antique item.

Potboiler

Q. *What is a "potboiler"?*

A. This term refers to something done only for the money, that is, *to keep the pot boiling*. The writer who turns out work of little or no originality just so he can earn a living may be said to be producing "potboilers."

Contributor's Copies

Q. *Is not the phrase, "Payment in contributor's copies" ambiguous? Does it not mean "payment in copies to contributors"?*

A. "Contributor's copies" is a term that is generally taken to mean copies of the issue in which the contributor's work appears.

Kill Fee

Q. *What is a "kill fee"? When is it used?*

A. Kill fee is a fee paid to a writer who has worked on an assignment which, for one reason or another, was not published. The writer, for example, is asked (assigned) to write a 3,000-word article, but after he does the research and writes the 3,000 words, the editor decides—for some reason—that the piece will not be published after all. The writer is then given a percentage (usually 20% of the purchase price offered for the full manuscript) as a kill fee. The 20% kill fee is flexible, depending on the publication's policy. It may range from ten percent to higher than 20%. Kill fees aren't too common, and are usually offered only to professional writers. It's rare that an editor would offer a kill fee, for example, to a writer whose work is not familiar to him, or to a writer who hasn't previously worked for him. The writer is, after receiving the kill fee, permitted to submit the article to other markets for possible sale. Remember, though, that the writer does not ordinarily receive a kill fee unless mention of it is included in the original assignment.

Book Packager

Q. *What is a "book packager"?*

A. A "book packager" makes contracts with publishers to find writers to do specific writing projects. The packager usually signs a contract with a publisher and then a different one with the writer based on what he thinks he can get the writer to do the work for, and what the writer thinks he's worth for that particular job.

Manual of Style

Q. *I've seen the Chicago* Manual of Style *referred to often by editors. Just what is it and where can I find a copy?*

A. The Chicago *Manual of Style* is a book which refers to the manner of preparing a manuscript according to the style guidelines developed by the University of Chicago, published in an extensive volume by them. It gives guidelines for capitalization, punctuation, italicization, etc. You can probably see a copy at the reference department in your local library, or order a copy directly from the University of Chicago Press, 5801 Ellis Ave., Chicago 60637. Price of last edition was $12.50.

Types of Fiction

Q. *Could you please explain what you mean by "genre" fiction? An editor said that's the kind of fiction he buys, and I've never seen any reference to it before now. Also explain "experimental" and "mainstream" and the differences between them.*

A. Genre fiction, sometimes called category fiction, includes stories that can be easily labeled, such as science fiction, fantasy, mystery, suspense, Gothic, Western and erotica. Mainstream—the type of fiction that most often becomes a bestseller—does not comfortably fit into the above categories. Mainstream fiction employs conventional techniques to tell the story, while experimental fiction is unconventional. Experimental novelists share a common interest in form—style, structure, symbol, narrative technique—over and above the development of the "story." Beginning writers are usually urged to follow the traditional route for their first attempts, since markets for experimental fiction are limited.

Types of Nonfiction

Q. *There is a series of terms that appears in magazine market information that I'm not sure I understand. One reason may be that I have never seen a list of comparative definitions for them. I would appreciate such definitions and comparison—showing, if possible, any clear cut differences between the following terms: articles, essays, features, "new journalism."*

A. Articles are always nonfiction—accounts of real things happening, or things that have happened already; they can be informational, how-to, personal experience, interviews, profiles, inspirational, humor, historical, think articles, expose, nostalgia, personal opinion, photo articles, travel, successful business operations articles, new product articles, merchandising technique articles, and technical articles. Essays are written compositions, usually personal in tone; giving one's personal opinion or ideas on a given topic. Features are articles, usually with human interest, giving the reader background information on the news. The term "feature" is sometimes used by magazine editors to indicate a lead article or distinctive department in their publication. In other words, a feature article may be the article given most importance in a particular issue of the magazine. "New journalism" is article writing using many fiction techniques; it's a form of journalism that also involves the writer's own feelings about his subject as opposed to "objective" journalism.

Tear Sheets

Q. *If you quote a title and some verses from a song in a short story (with permission, of course) and the publishing company who holds the copyright asks for a "tear sheet" if the story is published, what exactly is it that you send?*

A. If and when the story is published, you would simply clip (or "tear") out the pages on which this material appears in the magazine and send them to the publisher who requested "tear sheets."

Filler Markets

Q. *I would like to know what is meant by fillers. Where would a writer get this material?*

A. Fillers mean what their name implies. They may be crossword puzzles, newspaper clips, short featurettes, poetry, brief anecdotes, sayings, etc., that are used to fill up the empty spaces left in the magazine layout after the regular features have been placed in position. The type of filler would depend on the slant and makeup of the magazine. Fillers may either be original or they may be quoted from other sources. In the case of the latter, the original source and date of publication is indicated by the writer when submitting. Hundreds of the magazines buying fillers describe their needs in WRITER'S MARKET.

Pedestrian Writing

Q. *Several times I have come across literary criticism using the phrase "pedestrian writing." The phrase has been used in discussing published material without stating whether it is considered good writing. Exactly what is "pedestrian writing" and what makes it so?*

A. The term "pedestrian," when applied to writing, is definitely unflattering. It means the work is prosaic or dull. The Latin root "ped-" refers to the foot, and of course the usual definition of the noun "pedestrian" is: one who travels on foot ... such as the common man (who presumably doesn't have a fancier way to travel). In connection with writing, the adjective then would mean common or ordinary.

Newspaper Stringers

Q. *What is the definition of the word "stringer" as used in the following ad: "Newspaper chain has opening for editor and also has openings for stringers in all sections of the country"? Are they the same as correspondents or different?*

A. Yes, a stringer is a local correspondent whose job it is to keep his regional newspaper supplied with items concerning his particular community. The term is an old newspaper one that derives from the fact that a local correspondent's copy was strung together, measured, and then paid for by the inch. If you're interested in learning more about stringers, read the article entitled "How to be a Small Town Stringer," by Reinhart Wessing, in Aron Mathieu's *The Creative Writer* (Writer's Digest Books).

"Quality" Magazine

Q. *What is a "quality magazine"?*

A. Specifically, *Atlantic, Harper's, Esquire, Saturday Review,* etc. The magazines in this "quality" group have high literary standards and are interested in the artistic merit of the writer and his ability to express himself in a sensitive and individualistic manner. Fiction is usually of the nonformula type, and the emphasis is frequently on characterization and insight into human emotion and behavior rather than on the intricacies of plotting.

Those Trade Terms!

Q. *What is a "think piece"? Does it mean a controversial article? Or does it mean all kinds of nonfiction? Even a historical piece, non-controversial, will cause me to think—and doubtless most other readers.*

A. A "think piece" is usually any article that has an intellectual, philosophical, provocative approach to its subject.

Mailing Services

Q. *What does "mailing and remailing" mean in the ads in* Writer's Digest?

A. A mailing service agency mails an author's work from its own locality when the author travels frequently or prefers a postmark that does not reveal his place of residence.

Belles Lettres

Q. *What does the category "belles lettres" cover? I've seen it in several of the market listings, and would like an explanation.*

A. The dictionary definition of "belles lettres" is literally "fine letters" —literature that is an end in itself and not practical or purely informative. This would seem to include all fiction, but in practice it includes only the finer works of writers which literary critics have acclaimed as superior.

Story or Article?

Q. *When a story is based on an actual happening, but polished up to a degree, should it be called a story or an article? In today's writing, the dividing line between fiction and fact is so narrow it is hard to distinguish between them.*

A. If a story is told only from the narrator's viewpoint and the incidents are factually accurate and based on a true personal experience, the story would probably be considered nonfiction.

"Newsbreak"?

Q. *What are "newsbreaks"?*

A. A "newsbreak" to most editors is simply a newsworthy event or item. For example, an opening of a new retail shoe store in a town might be a "newsbreak" for a shoe trade journal that publishes news items of new openings. Some publications (such as *The New Yorker*) use "newsbreak" in a different sense—that is, to indicate a typo or an error in reporting that appears in a printed news story. Such "newsbreaks"—followed by tongue-in-cheek editorial commentary—are bought from contributors and used in *The New Yorker* and other publications as filler items.

Writing in "Depth"

Q. *Would you explain the term "depth" in the field of writing?*

A. "Depth" would naturally mean many things to many editors. But perhaps the one interpretation they would all agree on is that a piece of writing that has depth has something important to say to readers. It would avoid frivolity or top-of-the-head superficiality about the ideas presented; it would require thought on the part of the writer *and* the reader. Nonfiction of depth would be based on well-researched data. Fiction of depth would arise from thoughtful sensitivity to and perception of human behavior.

Amateur vs. Professional

Q. *When editors say they want professionally written or sophisticated material, what do they mean?*

A. They mean they want the type of writing that represents a polished use of the language plus skillfully developed treatment of the subject. Flaws in grammar and word choice, lacklustre style, sloppy plotting or research, poor organization, absence of a point, are all signs of the amateur rather than the professional. The demand for sophisticated material rules out anything trite or corny but suggests a desire for a certain degree of wit and subtlety that would appeal to readers who are intellectually sharp about the significance of the world around them.

Proofreading

Q. *What is "proofreading" and how can a beginning writer learn to proofread?*

A. Proofreading usually applies to reading a printer's proof of your article, story or book to correct any typographical errors. A beginning writer can learn to proofread by studying the standard proofreader's marks and using them in earlier drafts of his own manuscript to help him in retyping final copy. See the appendix in this book for a list of standard proofreading symbols.

2. Education for Writers

Education

Q. *Is it necessary to take a course in writing to become a successful writer? How valuable is a college education or at least some college training to a writer? Is a good noncollege correspondence course from a reputable writer's school sufficient? I am interested primarily in fiction and feature writing.*

A. Creative writing courses, whether at college or through a reputable correspondence school, are valuable in helping the beginning writer master fundamental techniques, polish his style, and gain insight through constructive authoritative criticism of his work. Writing courses are also helpful in teaching a writer to be disciplined, which is important for writing success. Such courses are not sufficient in themselves, though. A broad general education, whether acquired formally at college or informally by other means, is necessary, too.

Evaluation of Correspondence Schools

Q. *How can a writer evaluate correspondence courses across the nation? I would like to look into all the writing correspondence courses that are offered, and was wondering if there has been a study of them or any statistics, etc. What about Writer's Digest School?*

A. There is no national rating service for correspondence schools. Most reputable ones, however, are registered and licensed in their own state, as Writer's Digest School is in Ohio. By writing to the state board of school and college registration you can get an honest evaluation of the school in which you are interested. (Writer's Digest School's number is #73-10-0409H.) If you wish to write to the State of Ohio, address your letter to Executive Secretary, State Board of School & College Registration, 88 E. Broad St., Columbus, Ohio 43215. WD School offers courses on various types of writing—short story, article writing, confession story writing, and writing short stories or novels for young people. Instructors for the school are all professional writers or editors who have expertise in their field. The instruction is on a one-to-one basis and each student keeps the same instructor for the length of his course. For more information on WD School, write Kirk Polking, Director, 9933 Alliance Rd., Cincinnati 45242.

Grammar Phobia

Q. *I am a "would-be" writer; that is, I believe I could write salable material if I could only get rid of one great big fear—the fear of punctuation! Just how important is punctuation to the sale of a story or article? I have read and studied the English grammars till I feel positively hopeless when I can't remember the rules a minute after I've closed the book. I'm desperate when I can't recall the rule for using a semicolon, a period, a comma, or when to start a new paragraph. I waste too much time trying to decide where a comma goes, whether to use a semicolon, or start a new sentence. Like I said, I can't remember the rules! Are all writers expert grammarians? Should I let this fear stop me from trying to write?*

A. You have let punctuation become more of a bugaboo than it really should be for you. Notice your punctuation in this very letter ... it's quite acceptable. You probably used common sense as your guide. You properly allowed a semicolon to separate two principal clauses. You used the comma to indicate pauses in a train of thought and to separate the words in a series. You used the period to denote the end of a statement. Since you're allergic to books of rules, perhaps you would do better to work with stories published in current magazines. Become aware of the function of punctuation by seeing how it's used in each case. By all means, continue to write and never let your fear of literary mechanics scare you off. If the talent is there, it will be recognized regardless of whether every comma is in the right place.

Journalism Departments

Q. *Could you tell me the rank or list of the top ten or 15 journalism departments in our universities?*

A. There is no definitive list concerning the academic standing in journalism. However, your public library undoubtedly has the booklet, "Accredited Programs in Journalism," (American Council on Education for Journalism). It lists, in alphabetical order, all the accredited schools and departments of Journalism on the college level. For additional information, address your inquiry to: Secretary-Treasurer, American Council on Education for Journalism, School of Journalism, U. of Missouri, Columbia, Missouri 65201.

"Best" Creative Writing School?

Q. *Can you send me a listing of the best creative writing schools for would-be novelists?*

A. The "best" creative writing school for you would depend on what you expect from it, how much you can afford to pay, your own talents, and many other factors. A list of colleges throughout the U.S. which have Creative Writing departments, or at least offer some creative writing courses, can be obtained from Associated Writing Programs, c/o Washington College, Chestertown, Maryland 21620.

Fellowships, Grants

Q. *I would appreciate it if you would direct me to a list of known literary fellowships and grants, connected with publishers, colleges, etc. Also, is there a directory of foundation grants?*

A. Lists of private and government foundations that are of interest to writers are: *Grants and Awards Available to American Writers,* 9th edition, $2 (PEN American Center, 156 Fifth Ave., New York City 10010); *Grants and Aid to Individuals in the Arts,* 3rd edition, $13.95 (Washington International Arts Letter, 1321 Fourth St. S.W., Washington D.C. 20024); *Arts Support by Private Foundations,* Vol. 3, $45 in paper (Washington International Arts Letter); and *Study Abroad,* $7.50 (if prepaid) plus sales tax (UNESCO, 650 First Ave., New York City 10016).

Scholarships and Loans

Q. *I am a high school Senior planning to enter a college next fall. The field I am interested in is journalism. Would you please give me information on journalism pertaining to scholarships and loans?*

A. There is a *Journalism Scholarship Guide* published by the Newspaper Fund, P.O. Box 300, Princeton, New Jersey 08540.

3. Getting Started in Freelancing

Making Your Debut

Q. *How do authors usually write and publish their first article?*

A. It normally happens one of two ways. The author picks a topic—one that greatly interests him and he feels he can write well—writes the piece and then tries to find a magazine to publish it. Or he studies a magazine he's personally interested in, to discover ideas for articles that would interest the editor of that magazine. He then queries that editor asking for an expression of interest in the article idea, or he prepares the article manuscript and submits it without querying first.

Shortcuts To Writing Success?

Q. *I am in great distress over the marketing of articles and short stories. Apparently, my four years of Liberal Arts plus three national writer's conventions is not enough. I just don't publish. Even my prize-winning short story has received six rejection slips. Are there shortcuts writers must know in order to publish? How does one sell more writing? How do you get a "yes" from editors? What are the markets for short stories?*

A. There really are no sure shortcuts to getting published—besides strictly adhering to editorial and submission requirements of the various markets. Some people think a shortcut might be to "know someone on the inside," but that usually doesn't help. The only way to sell more writing is to do more writing, to circulate more of your material, to be persistent. How do you get a "yes" from editors? By sending them exactly the kind of material they're looking for on that particular day, or by sending them something so fresh, so new, so exciting that they can't wait to share it with their readers. What are the markets for short stories? Check through the Consumer Magazines section of WRITER'S MARKET and The Markets column in WRITER'S DIGEST for specific names, addresses and editorial requirements. The market for short stories is not dead—it's very much alive. To sell, you need to write short stories for a particular audience, for a special magazine. To know this audience you must study the magazine's back issues, including editorial matter and advertisements (which reveal plenty of information about persons who buy the publication).

Getting Started, Getting a "Name"

Q. *I've been writing for my local newspaper, without pay, for several years. When I try to query a national magazine, I have no published credits to list. I've run into the problem of people not granting me an interview because I have no credits, and they feel it's wasting their time to let me interview them. Even when I get a "go-ahead" from an editor I've queried, I find people hesitant to give me their time for an interview. How do you suggest I get started in the national market, and how can I get my name before readers other than those that read the local newspaper?*

A. You *do* have published credits—in your local newspaper. Sometimes being published in the newspaper helps, even if you don't get paid, because it gives you valuable experience. You can tell editors and potential interviewees you've been published in the local *Times Herald* and they will be impressed. And so will those people you want to interview. If they are hesitant to grant the interview—be persistent. Don't let them say "no." Landing your first interview may be tough, but the experience you gain will make those interviews that follow much easier.

The Freelancer

Q. *When is a person considered a freelance writer? Someone told me if I had at least one article published that I was considered a freelance writer. Is this true?*

A. Freelance means that the person is self-employed as a writer and is not on the salaried staff of any one newspaper, magazine or publishing house. Some writers who have published little still consider themselves freelancers because they are working on their own and submitting to the markets of their choice. The professional's viewpoint is that a true freelance writer earns a substantial part of his income from his writing.

Reviews

Q. *I'd like to get started in theater and movie criticism, but don't know where to begin. Are there any shortcuts to the field?*

A. One way beginners get started in theater and movie criticism or review is by writing sample pieces and sending them to newspapers in their area that don't have a staff critic. The newspapers sometimes can be persuaded to take the beginner on as a stringer.

4. Preparing the Manuscript

Word Count

Q. *Does it make a difference in what I'm paid if I don't include the word count on a manuscript when I submit it? Might I get paid more if I add it?*

A. Most editors prefer to have the approximate word count noted on the upper right-hand corner of page one of the manuscript. However, that will have no bearing on the purchase price of the manuscript. It makes no difference in the amount you receive for the article or story.

One, Two, Three ...

Q. *I have never learned how writers arrive at the total number of words in a manuscript. Can you tell me?*

A. Count every word on five representative pages; divide by five to get an average number of words per page and then multiply that average by the total number of pages in the manuscript. When counting words, abbreviated words count as one word as does the word "a," "the," etc. Show approximate number of words in round figures, such as 2,700 words (not 2,693) in the upper right-hand corner of page one.

Retype Again?

Q. *Is it essential that a manuscript be neat? I have a 480-page manuscript that I've retyped three times and it's still a mess. Every time I retype it, I reread it, which is disastrous because my pen flies with revisions (usually of words, not sentences). If I retype it again, I'll be wasting weeks that could be used in creating. Or should I send it out with the "neat" word-substitutes.*

A. Since you can't resist revising every time you retype, you would probably find a professional manuscript typist the answer to your problem. The cost of this service would be worth the considerable saving in time and effort. Under no circumstances should you send out a manuscript that has more than three corrections marked on it, "neat" or not. Also to save wear and tear on the finished product, send the publisher a query letter first instead of submitting the complete manuscript.

Dot or Dashes

Q. *Is there any current guide with editorial sanction for the use of the three ...'s and the—? If so I would appreciate being let in on it.*

A. There is no strict editorial policy governing the use of the three ...'s and the—. In popular magazines such as *McCall's, Esquire, Argosy, New Yorker* and *Redbook* the dash seems to be more prevalent than the dots, though most of the magazines do use both, sometimes in the same story. The dots are used mainly to indicate that the speaker's voice trails off ...; the dash is used sometimes in place of parentheses or sometimes to indicate an abrupt interruption in speech or thought or to suggest a pause longer than a comma but not as final as a period. The dots are also used to show omission of words from a quote; e.g., *Senator John L. McGee said "We must examine closely ... the effect of postal rate increases on the magazine industry."* This statement could have appeared in a magazine industry newsletter where the omitted words *"agriculture grants, education proposals, and,"* would have been of little interest to the readers of the newsletter.

Writing Mechanics

Q. *I have often read the term "manuscript mechanics." Would you please tell me what this means?*

A. This term refers to the business of making a manuscript as attractive as possible from the standpoint of overall appearance. It entails neatness of typing, punctuation, width of margins, centering of titles, etc.

Pen Name

Q. *Could you tell me how one indicates on a manuscript that he is writing under a pseudonym?*

A. Your real name should appear on the upper left-hand corner of each page of your manuscript. But if you're determined to keep your identity a secret from your readers, then on the title page, use your pseudonym in the byline. Of course, if you don't want even your editor or publisher to know your real name, then you'll have to be a little trickier and use the pseudonym in the byline, in the upper left-hand corner *and* on the return envelope. In this case, you'll have to notify your local post office and bank of this name change.

Credits for Quotes

Q. *Where should quotation credits be given in a manuscript—at the bottom of the page where it appears or at the end of the manuscript?*

A. Usually credits are given by placing an asterisk next to the quote and a corresponding asterisk and notation of credits at the bottom of the page.

Testimonials

Q. *Clifford Beers' book,* A Mind That Found Itself, *had many letters by famous people praising his work and book. I believe these letters were one of the factors that made his book such a success. Would you advise me to type an extra copy or two of the book I'm writing and send it to various people for similar letters to be printed in my book?*

A. The garnering of letters of praise from famous people will usually be taken care of by the publisher's publicity department. Remember that you haven't yet obtained a contract for the book you're working on, so wait until the publisher accepts your manuscript before discussing testimonials with him. After acceptance, if you have in mind some specific persons who you think would respond favorably to your book, suggest them to the publisher.

Date Style

Q. *In my writing, I often need to refer to the days and months of the year, omitting the year. It is correct, is it not, to use ordinal numerals to designate the days, for example: January 12th, May 1st, March 5th?*

A. The accepted practice is as follows: January 12, May 1, March 5.

Religious Manuscript

Q. *Will you please tell me where I could send a religious manuscript to be read and edited? It is one my father wrote before his death in 1961. I found it some time ago and read it and feel it is good enough to be published. It is mimeographed and is single-spaced (approximately 9,500 words). Would I have to retype this and double-space it?*

A. Yes, if you want your father's manuscript to have a proper reading at an editorial office, it will have to be retyped, double-spaced on 8½x11 paper. Since its length of 9,500 words is too long for an article in a magazine and too short for a book, marketing it as is may be a problem. When retyping it, you might see how it could be cut and edited for a magazine. A list of religious magazines appears in WRITER'S MARKET.

Underline for Italics

Q. *I am working on a short story in which short paragraphs in italics are interspersed throughout the narrative, and would like to know whether there is any way to indicate italics without underlining. This amounts to quite extensive underlining, which, in my opinion, is not only bothersome and time consuming but is distracting to the reader. A beginning writer cannot afford to distract an editor any more than he can help!*

A. Underlining *is* the standard way to denote italics; editors would not be any more distracted by it than readers would be by the actual italics.

Children's Story

Q. *I would like to know if I am preparing my manuscripts of children's stories in the most favorable manner. I type them as I would any short story, without illustrations and without any suggestions or indications for same.*

A. Yes, your presentation is acceptable. Leave the matter of illustration to the publisher who buys the story.

Which Type?

Q. *I have only one typewriter and it has elite type. I know when manuscripts are submitted that pica is preferred. But does it make that much difference?*

A. Relax, both pica and elite are acceptable. The more "exotic" types, such as fancy script or all capitals, are what editors find objectionable.

When to Hyphenate

Q. *What is the fundamental rule, if there is one, about hyphenated words?*

A. If you consult the introductory pages of most standard un-abridged dictionaries, you will find rules pertaining to the use of hy-phens. Rules *can* get to be rather complicated. But a few simple ones to bear in mind are that the hyphen can be used (1) to clarify mean-ing, e.g., honey-child ... not a child made of honey; (2) to avoid having a double vowel or a triple consonant, e.g., wall-like is prefera-ble to walllike; (3) to aid proper pronunciation, e.g., all-embracing is less likely to be mispronounced than allembracing. In general, just remember that if the hyphen helps to make your meaning clearer, use it.

Novel Preparation

Q. *I am embarking on a novel and need to know the following: Is it single- or double-spaced? Is there a margin to consider? Is the average novel from 60,000 to 80,000 words? Should I send a query or com-plete manuscript? Should I use bond paper?*

A. Double-space your manuscript, leaving about a one-inch margin all around. Various publishers have different word requirements (see WRITER'S MARKET listings under Book Publishers), but many of the novels do fall into the 60-80,000 word group. Use standard 8½x11 typewriter bond paper. Instead of mailing the whole manuscript, first send out a synopsis plus two or three sample chapters and a let-ter asking if the publisher is interested. Be sure to include postage and an envelope for the return of your material.

Thoughts in Quotes?

Q. *I have been told that thoughts should not be enclosed in quotation marks. This works very well in some cases, but there are instances in which I do not know how to handle the punctuation, as in the following: Jim said, "Walter is a wonderful fellow." Alice agreed and thought, "You are wonderful too." Should quotation marks be used in this case, and if not, should "You" begin with a capital letter?*

A. Quotation marks need not be used here, but the capital letter for "You" should be retained. Or, if the use of a capital in the middle of a sentence disturbs you, you might handle it this way: Alice agreed. You are wonderful too, she thought. If you like you may underscore her thought to indicate italics, which would differentiate it nicely from the direct quotations.

Quotation Credits

Q. *I am writing a textbook. In places, for a line or so, I quote either from* Webster's Dictionary *or an encyclopedia; in others I use their material but reword it to make it simple for a child to understand. Will it be sufficient, at the end of the book, to give references used without listing each single place in which they are used?*

A. You may safely reword the reference book material to make it understandable to children. And although it is usually necessary to request permission to quote from copyrighted material, in your case your quotations would undoubtedly come under the principles of "fair use" which legally allow *brief* quotations for scholarly purposes. Correct acknowledgment of the source material as you propose should be acceptable.

Triple-Space?

Q. *I triple-space on manuscripts rather than double-space because my typewriter has elite (small) type. Is this acceptable to magazine editors or do they always prefer double-spacing?*

A. Double-spacing is preferable but triple-spacing would probably be acceptable to magazine editors. You'll just have to try it and see.

How Long?

Q. *Can you help me? I need to know how many words will make an average radio story of 60 minutes?*

A. Radio feature copy usually runs 15 double-spaced lines to equal one minute or about two pages to equal three minutes. The crux of the matter, of course, is how fast the narrator speaks.

The End or -30-

Q. *I have a question pertaining to both novels and short stories. Should you put "The End" at the end? I've seen "30" in some places, indicating the ending of the manuscript (both for fiction and nonfiction). Which is correct?*

A. You can write "The End" at the end of both a short story and a novel, although you don't have to—it isn't a fast rule that you do. The number "30" is usually written at the end of copy for nonfiction, most often used in newspaper stories and reports. It is a legacy from old newspaper telegraphers who used the Roman numeral XXX as a symbol to indicate the end of the message.

Subtitles Included?

Q. *In many magazine articles there are subtitles placed between paragraphs to attract the reader's attention to a change in thought. Should a writer put these in the manuscript or is this an editorial procedure?*

A. This is usually an editorial procedure. The editor may want them placed in certain locations both for editorial emphasis and/or to help a layout paste-up problem. Writers need not include subtitles (also called subheads) in the original manuscript submitted; however, if an editor requests an author to include subtitles, or to suggest suitable subtitles, the writer should do that.

The Cover Letter

Q. *I have been thrust into the position of "agent" and I need help! The book I've been asked to market is a good one (it's an exposé) and I have confidence in its salability. I know that since it is nonfiction, I need only send to prospective publishers two or three chapters, a table of contents, and the author's credentials. What I don't know is how to present myself as an agent. I am not familiar with book contracts or with agents' shop talk. Just what do I say in my covering letter?*

A. Although to practice professionally as an agent you would need experience as a marketer (see chapter on Author's Agents) you could have some letterheads printed which include your name, address, and an identifying phrase such as Author's Representative. Simply write a covering letter to the prospective publisher, indicating what you're enclosing on behalf of your client and why you think it's a good prospect for that firm, its market potential, and so on. If you're eligible to join the Author's Guild—because you've published a book or written for national magazines—do so, so that you can get their sample book contract with recommended clauses, etc. The Society of Author's Representatives (101 Park Ave., New York City 10017) sells a sample book contract for 75¢ (send coins or stamps only, no checks). Get one, but keep in mind that contracts will vary from publisher to publisher. The amount of the advance and terms of subsidiary rights will also vary depending on whether the book author is a first-time writer or a well-established professional with a "name." Read *Publishers Weekly* to see what books are being published by whom and what kind of sales can be expected.

Children's Books

Q. *My husband and I are writing and illustrating a book for children. What media are used for children's book illustrations and how are the illustrations submitted?*

A. If your book is accepted, the publisher will probably have his own ideas about how it should be illustrated, so prepare a few sample illustrations only, until you get an okay from a publisher. You might want to read the chapters on Illustration and Production, however, in the book, *Writing, Illustrating and Editing Children's Books,* by Jean P. Colby.

Erasable Bond

Q. *Please set me straight once and for all. Half the time I read that manuscripts should be prepared on non-Corrasable paper because it smudges less, and the other half of the time they say that liquid erase should be avoided, and that a good eraser is best. This leads me to believe that neither is a steadfast rule. I would, however, appreciate knowing what the general consensus is.*

A. It's general knowledge that erasable bond is an "editing nuisance." Most editors prefer good quality bond paper, and the use of either liquid erase, or strike-over erase. If you have more than three corrections on a manuscript page, though, it's best to retype that page—and avoid the first-draft look that editors are impatient with.

5. Finding the Facts

Library Research

Q. *In doing research in libraries for story material, copying long passages is a slow laborious job. Is there any known method that is faster?*

A. Talk to your local librarian about the availability of copying machines (such as Xerox) or perhaps about photostating the material you need.

Historical References

Q. *I am writing a short story based on a colorful but for the most part unheard of, or forgotten, figure of the 1820s. I studied a dozen or more library references to get the information I needed. How should I give credit without typing half a page to list my source of knowledge?*

A. In order to give credit where it is due and provide your story with the proper authentication, you should include, for the editor, a bibliography of source material even though it might take up "half a page."

Poetry Reference

Q. *I have just written a novel and am about to submit it to a publisher. My title is taken from a stanza learned many years ago; but I am unable to locate the source or author.*

A. You might try searching this out through either the *Poetry Index* or the *Essay and General Literature Subject Index* in your local public library.

Government Addresses

Q. *Presently, I am researching a highly controversial article which requires positive statistical support from numerous government agencies. It is important that the agencies give the information, "from the horse's mouth," for record purposes. Where exactly, may I get the correct mail address of the parent departments and subordinate bureaus of the government?*

A. The *United States Government Manual* is probably in your local library. This publication will give you the current addresses of the various departments and bureaus of the government.

Permission to Include

Q. *In doing a "round-up" article should I have the consent of the individuals whom I include if the information is gathered by other than personal interview? What I have in mind are actors with some background trait in common, etc. Also, is it professional to interview by mail when your subject is out of your local vicinity?*

A. Yes, it is best to have the consent of the individuals whom you would include in a "round-up" article. Yes, many writers do interview by mail or phone when the subject is out of their local vicinity.

Reference Source

Q. *I would appreciate any information that you may have concerning children's periodicals—their history, development, uses, etc.*

A. If you will check in your local library for a directory called the *Subject Guide to Books in Print,* there, under Children's Literature—History and Criticism, you will find a number of books listed that may be of help to you.

Sunrise? Sunset?

Q. *I have lived in many different places in the U.S. and also briefly overseas. Sometimes I like to use these various places as settings, but I find it very difficult to remember the hours of sunset and sunrise. Is there a book that lists such facts?*

A. The exact times would seem to be unimportant to any stories you might wish to write, but you can check in the *American Ephemeris and Nautical Almanac* which gives these times for every fifth day. You would, of course, have to first determine the latitude of your setting from a map.

Thank You Notes Necessary?

Q. *I am doing research for an article by writing letters to many companies across the country. Many have written detailed answers to me and given me much information that I might not otherwise have gotten. Is it customary or polite to answer each one of these with a thank you? This could run into quite a bit of correspondence for me, but I do feel that I owe these people some thanks for their co-operation. What do you say?*

A. Thank you notes are not obligatory in this case, but they would certainly be welcomed and appreciated. You may, if you wish, send the helpful companies tearsheets of your article when it's printed, along with a thank you for the information they contributed.

Books By Mail?

Q. *There are some books I'd like to read, but they're not in our local public library. Is there anyplace I can borrow these books so I don't have to buy a copy of each one?*

A. Most public libraries participate in a plan called inter-library loan. That is, if you want a book that your library does not have, they will borrow it from another library, charging you only the cost of postage required to get the book and return it. Ask you local librarian about this plan.

Problems With Organization

Q. *I need help on researching and organizing all my material before I actually sit down to write an article. I spend so much time shuffling papers around I never can get started writing.*

A. How the professionals do it is described in *A Treasury of Tips for Writers,* by the Society of Magazine Writers (Writer's Digest Books), along with their ideas on other subjects such as interviewing, keeping records, and, of course, writing.

Reference Source

Q. *How can I find out any information on Language Arts in the second and third grades?*

A. A public library near you probably has a reference book called *Subject Guide to Books in Print,* where you could find under the category "Language and Languages" some books that would be helpful.

Science Fiction Writing

Q. *Are there any books available pertaining to the writing of science fiction?*

A. Yes. For titles, see the *Subject Guide to Books in Print* under the categories: "Science Fiction—History and Criticism" and "Science Fiction—Technique." WRITER'S DIGEST has also published *Writing and Selling Science Fiction,* edited by C.L. Grant, which includes chapters by members of the Science Fiction Writers of America on markets, characters, dialog, "world-building," and other special problems of this genre. Many science fiction anthologies, too, contain introductions that offer insight into this specialized field.

Starting a Literary Paper

Q. *I'd like information about how to start a literary paper or magazine. Where can I learn more about this project?*

A. An organization which might offer you some specific suggestions is: Coordinating Council of Literary Magazines, 80 Eighth Ave., New York City 10011.

6. Questions About Querying

Query First?

Q. *I would like to ask about the "query first," which is always stressed. It seems so presumptuous for a beginning and unpublished writer to query first—how much attention would be paid them, anyway? I haven't yet had the nerve to try it.*

A. A busy editor would much rather read a query to decide whether he's interested in a certain property than plow through a lengthy manuscript for the same purpose. From the writer's standpoint, think of the savings in postage and wear-and-tear on the manuscript. What *is* presumptuous is the writer who disregards an editor's stated request to "query first" and deluges him with completed manuscripts.

Query for Short Stories?

Q. *When the market listing states "query," does that include short stories of 1,000 to 4,000 words?*

A. While "query" usually refers to nonfiction only, it will sometimes refer to fiction that is submitted to a market also. In the paragraph giving the market's fiction requirements, if it doesn't indicate "query for fiction," it's better to submit the complete story, rather than query first. Though it is rare that an editor would prefer a query for fiction, it does occasionally happen, and should be followed as a strict editorial requirement. Reasons for querying for fiction are usually that a market is inundated with fiction submissions, and the editor would prefer to see something of the writer's story line or ideas for stories before reading the entire manuscript.

Book Query

Q. *I am writing a novel and hope to have it ready to submit by early June. I looked in* WRITER'S MARKET *for names and addresses of book publishers, and a few things confused me. What is a book query? Is it a letter? Is it an informal outline? How long is it? What elements of a book does the query cover? Some publishers want you to send a complete manuscript, while others want an outline and a query. If the publisher doesn't say in his editorial listing how to submit manuscripts, then how should you submit them?*

A. A book query is a letter setting forth the contents of the book— usually a nonfiction book—by enclosing a summary or chapter outline, and indicating the market you see for the book. If a publisher indicates a cover or query letter should be sent with sample chapters, send a covering letter describing the market for your book, along with an outline and 50 sample pages so they can see your writing style. If the publishing company doesn't indicate a specific preference, you might do well to query first, enclosing the above items.

No Answer on a Query

Q. *If I send a query letter on an article idea to an editor and I don't get a reply, does that mean he's not interested?*

A. No, the letter may have been lost. Be sure to enclose a SASE with your query and, if you don't hear from the editor within a couple weeks, don't hesitate to write a brief follow-up asking whether he's had time to consider your proposal.

7. Using Quotes

News Item Quote

Q. *I have read poetry written in response to a line from a magazine or newspaper in which the line is quoted above the poem. Is it necessary to obtain permission from the original source in order to quote the line?*

A. If a line is simply part of a straight news item, no permission is needed. One line of copyrighted material is usually considered "fair use," except when the line is from an extremely short work, such as a poem.

TV Broadcast Quote

Q. *Will you please explain the rules governing the use by writers of quotes and information gained from TV broadcasts? As a feature writer with an extensive clipping file, I have taken notes on some programs and speakers covering topics on which I am collecting information and leads into further research.*

A. Generally speaking, if you accurately attribute your information to the proper source, you shouldn't run into any legal difficulty. In the case of direct quotations of *any length,* it might be best to write to the network or to the speaker, requesting permission to use the particular quotes.

Well-known Quote

Q. *In an original poem, I have said, "Good will upon earth, peace among men," which is based on the well-quoted phrase, "Peace on earth, good will to men." Is this legal?*

A. The line you're paraphrasing is already in the public domain, so you don't have to worry on *that* score. For other phrases that might have trademark protection, it would be advisable to reword the basic idea in your own way.

Stealing from Yourself

Q. *Would you please discuss the ethics involved in an author's taking from one of his own published stories a sentence, a phrase, a simile, or anything for that matter—for use in another story.*

A. The only prohibition would be the risk of having some alert readers tag you as belonging to that *New Yorker* category known as "Writers In Love With Their Own Words" department!

Government Publications

Q. *To quote from publications of the U.S. Department of Labor, Commerce, Bureau of Standards, do I need permission from that Department?*

A. Government publications (except a few allowed the Postmaster General) cannot be copyrighted, so you could quote freely—unless you are quoting already copyrighted material which happened to be part of a government publication. Look for the copyright notice to be sure.

Quoting Songs

Q. *If you only mention the title, do you have to have permission from the song publisher? And what about old songs you quote from* *memory, like ballads or nursery rhymes, etc.? Must you find a publisher then and ask his permission? I plan to use quotes from some old lumberjack ballads and a few songs popular 15 or ten years ago. I don't think a music store could help much on songs that old, could it?*

A. You may mention a song title without having to get the song publisher's permission. As for old familiar folk ballads and nursery rhymes, if they are all older than 1909 they are in the public domain and can be used by anyone, without permission. In the case of songs popular about 15 years ago, however, their copyright will not likely have run out yet (length of copyright protection prior to 1978 is 28 years, with renewal for another 28 years) so you probably need permission. Check for the publisher of popular songs by title in a directory available in most public libraries called the *Variety Music Cavalcade.*

Paraphrasing

Q. *Must I write for permission from the copyright holder in order to paraphrase material, as with quoted material? When quoting from another book, may I omit surplus words such as "the," abbreviate or engage in other editing without using distracting dots to indicate such minor deletions?*

A. No permission is needed for paraphrased passages, though sources of ideas should be acknowledged. The fact that a verbatim quote has been edited should, in all fairness, be indicated primarily to show readers that this is not exactly the way the author wrote it. The use of dots is the accepted practice, and not usually considered distracting.

Brief Quotes for Reviews Without Permission

Q. *Many books have statements similar to the following: All rights reserved. No part of this book may be reproduced in any form without written permission from the publisher, except for brief passages included in a review appearing in a newspaper or magazine. May brief passages be quoted by reviewers in their reviews from books that do not bear similar statements?*

A. Yes, even though books do not make this statement, reviewers may quote briefly from them under the "fair use" provision of the copyright law.

Request Permission

Q. *I write articles for various dental trade journals and sometimes I write to people in the field for opinions regarding methods. I explain my intentions of writing an article concerning the subject of the information I'm seeking. Is it OK to use their correspondence in my article, or must I ask for their permission to do so?*

A. Yes. Although the piece of paper on which a letter is written is the physical property of the recipient, the ideas expressed in it are still the property of the sender, and you must get permission to use the information from the letter in your article.

Slogans

Q. *I am writing a short story in which I am quoting excerpts from two major television commercials. I assume these advertisements are copyrighted. Is it necessary to obtain permission to use them?*

A. When in doubt, the safest rule is always to ask permission to quote. Although slogans can't be copyrighted, a trademark or patent can be registered for them.

Writing a Journal

Q. *I'm working on a 20th Century Journal-Notebook and would like to know how extensively I may quote from my reading (mostly contemporary fiction) without publisher's/writer's permission.*

A. This type of quoting may become a legal problem since it concerns an interpretation of what the copyright owners feel is "fair use." To be on the safe side, you should request permission to quote the particular passages you intend to use in your journal.

Using People's Names and Quotes

Q. *I've finished writing a novel of truth in fictional form, centered around the life of a doctor, and the book includes lots of facts and quotes. Names are mentioned in actual quotes. But I cannot give proper credit for some other items because my clippings of them were destroyed. How should I handle the use of people's names and quotes?*

A. If you're using actual names in your novel, you'd better make sure you have permission, in case one of those persons decides to sue you for invasion of privacy, even if whatever you are quoting is not libelous.

Getting Quotes from Experts

Q. *How can I get quotes from experts? Also how can I find incidents and examples to add substance to magazine articles I'm writing?*

A. After you've decided which experts you'd like to get quotes from, write them individual letters in care of their business addresses. Explain the subject matter of your article and the magazine for which you're writing, and ask your appropriate questions. Be sure to enclose SASE for the reply. As for finding incidents and examples—read a lot of other reference material on the same subject. Talk to people in your area who may have had experiences in the specific field you're writing about. Ask them to suggest other people in other parts of the country who may be able to help you.

8. Writing and Selling the Magazine Article

Resubmit?

Q. *I have written some articles that I would like to see in more than one magazine. When I write for religious papers, I do not ask for any pay for the articles. But I take several of these magazines myself and would like to send the articles to each one. Would this be legal? If these were paid for, would it be legal then to send to another editor?*

A. On future submissions, you might want to type in the upper right hand corner of page one of your manuscript: "Submitted on a non-exclusive basis at your regular rates." This tells the editor that he or she is not the only editor offered the manuscript. Many editors of religious magazines know that their readers are not likely to see the same article in another denomination's publication and are willing to accept these "simultaneous submissions." They may, however, choose to pay only a reprint price rather than the original article fee, which seems only fair under the circumstances.

Anecdotes

Q. *I need advice about use of anecdotes in articles. Do they have to be exactly from life to be ethical? How about making one up to suit the need?*

A. If you're going to mention the names of actual people, then you'd better stick to real-life facts. But if you want to make up an anecdote to illustrate a point in a nonfiction article, then you might preface it with something like: "It's the sort of town where something like the following could easily happen:—" ... or "There's a rumor going around that—" or "I wouldn't be surprised if—." You see, in this way the point can be made, but without giving the erroneous idea that the incident actually did take place. The secret of good anecdote-telling is the ability to spot a small true-life happening and describe it in such a way that your interpretation gives it new dimension and significance.

Recipe Sales

Q. *During a spring trip to the Pacific Northwest, I developed a form of "oven" camp cooking along with some special recipes. One recipe involves the use of six nationally known food products. I wish to achieve two objectives: 1) the presentation of the six-product recipe to the individual companies involved; 2) an illustrated article describing the "oven" cooking including all the recipes. How might I offer the recipes six separate times to the six companies? Could I then, if any one of them used the recipe, retain the rights to incorporate this six-product recipe in the article to be presented early next year to a magazine devoted to outdoor living and camping?*

A. You might be putting the dessert before the main dish here. You would do better *first* to write the article featuring the recipe. If and when it appears in that camping magazine, you could then send six copies of this published article to the six companies. These companies will no doubt be pleased to learn of this original use of their product, but do not expect any remuneration from them for this.

Published but Not Paid

Q. *An article of mine was published in a national magazine, and I've tried unsuccessfully to collect payment for it from the editor. I've written to him at least twice, sent one letter by registered mail asking payment and haven't been able to get a response although payment was promised on publication. I understand the Better Business Bureau can be notified, and in some cases, will give some help if it warrants. How do you go about that? What about suing for the payment?*

A. When you write the Better Business Bureau (BBB) to register a complaint about some unethical business practice, always write to the bureau in the state or city where the offender is located—in this case, the magazine's publishing address. Write the BBB, and the state's attorney general also. You can also try the Postal Service, which sometimes investigates such claims. If you have any other articles at that market for consideration, you should certainly write the editor, withdrawing them. Also send a letter with the information to WRITER's DIGEST. Include the name of the publication, dates of submission, acceptance and publication, and titles of manuscripts that were published and not paid for. Copies of your entire correspondence with the market are also helpful. Other than that, there's no recourse but to sue, and it's up to you whether you care enough about the ethics of the case to want to make your point at a financial loss to yourself because of legal fees—which may be extensive unless you can take your case to a nearby Small Claims Court. By telling WRITER's DIGEST the name of the offending market, though, you're in a position to help other writers avoid the same problem with that market.

9. Writing for Newspapers

Getting a Staff Job

Q. *What can a beginning writer do to get a job on a small newspaper staff?*

A. Try to place some freelance features with the specific newspaper you'd like to work for, so the editor can see that 1) you know what a good feature is, and 2) you write well. Also, try to supply them with news items from a section of their newspaper circulation area that is not well covered. Show them samples of your work that are similar to what they publish. For information on newspaper writing, see *Stalking the Feature Story,* by William Ruehlmann (Writer's Digest Books).

Newspaper Markets

Q. *I'd like to write newspaper articles, but where can I find a list of newspapers?*

A. The 500-page worldwide *Editor & Publisher Yearbook* lists dailies, weeklies, minority newspapers and feature agencies. Order it for $30 from *Editor & Publisher,* 575 Lexington Ave., New York City 10022, or look at a copy at your local public library or the library of a large daily newspaper. Annual editions come out in May. WRITER'S MARKET includes the category—Newspapers and Weekly Magazine Sections—which provides complete listings and editorial requirements for active newspaper markets for freelance material. *Ayer Directory of Publications* from Ayer Press, 210 W. Washington Sq., Philadelphia 19106, covers 22,800 newspapers, magazines and business, professional and trade journals, and sells for $54.89. These directories are available at most large public library reference departments.

Multiple Submissions to Newspapers

Q. *When submitting an article to more than one newspaper at a time (multiple submissions) is it necessary to let them know in specific wording that others—though not in the same city—will be getting the same material also?*

A. It might be a good idea to say "Exclusive in your circulation area" on multiple submissions to newspapers.

10. Interviewing Tips

Contacting a Celebrity

Q. *I'm a beginning writer and haven't sold anything yet. A singing celebrity is going to be in town in another month. Is it possible to arrange an interview with him? If so, how do I go about it?*

A. Contact the entertainment editor of your local newspaper to find out the name and address of the singer's manager. Write the manager and explain that you're a freelance writer and would like to interview the singer when he's in town. Name a specific magazine to whom you'd like to submit the interview (and if at all possible, get an expression of interest from its editor before you write the manager).

Tape Recorder Etiquette

Q. *I would like to use a tape recorder when I interview. Should I ask the interviewee beforehand if he minds, or should I simply plop it down without a word, turn it on, and proceed with the interview as if it didn't exist?*

A. It's more courteous to ask him first if he minds your using the tape recorder "to make sure you get his statements down as accurately as possible." Few will object. With experience you'll learn how to approach each interviewee with the idea. To learn how professional magazine writers have used the tape recorder in interviews, you might want to see their comments in *The Craft of Interviewing*, by John Brady (Writer's Digest Books).

Tell Subject He's Being Recorded?

Q. *I have a small gadget that records phone conversations without the other party's knowledge. Do I have to inform the person whom I'm interviewing that he is being taped?*

A. Many writers do not, since the real crux of the matter is what you *do* with the information you obtain in this manner. If, for example, an article you wrote was controversial and you were subsequently sued, it might create legal complications for you if it was learned that you had recorded a conversation without the subject's knowledge. On the other hand, if your interviewee is freely giving you information, and he knows that you're planning to use it in an article, there should be no problem.

Interviewing

Q. *I am interested in learning how to interview people—not just celebrities, but ordinary people too. I need their opinions and answers to questions for several articles I am working on. Do you just walk up to people and ask them? Do you have to have some sort of credentials? Do you need a release on the material they give you? Do you have to name them in an article, or are you not supposed to name them? Do you have to pay them?*

A. Yes, many freelance writers just walk up to people and ask them if they can interview them briefly for some research material they are seeking. No, writers do not usually pay the people they interview. No, it is not necessary to name them in the article unless they are authorities whom you are quoting and it would lend credence to your article to quote them specifically by name. If you do quote them specifically by name then, yes, you do need a release on the material they give you.

11. Submitting Photos With Manuscripts

Slides and Transparencies

Q. *I'm confused by the term "transparencies," which most editors use when discussing their requirements for color photos. Does it mean one thing to all editors, or does it mean slides to one editor and negatives to another?*

A. "Slides" and "transparencies" are terms used synonymously by most editors when referring to positive color film. "Negatives" usually refers to black-and-white (b&w) film only. Most editors will not work with color prints, developed from color negatives.

Picture Sources

Q. *In writing articles, I often need pictures for illustrations, and do not know where to get them. (I am not a photographer.) Of course, I should like them at a reasonable price or better still, free.*

A. For a list of free, or almost-free picture sources, see the book, *Picture Sources,* (Special Libraries Association). These photos can be used by themselves, or to supplement pictures shot specifically for your article by either a professional photographer you engaged for the purpose, or a photographer who has agreed to work with you on speculation.

Which Camera?

Q. *What is a good camera to take along to photograph an interviewee? Is an expensive one necessary?*

A. There are many good cameras on the market, priced from about $150 and up. You should first determine what your needs are. Will you be using the camera often? For what types of photos? (For photos to accompany an interview, for example, you would need just one standard lens, and maybe a flash attachment, but for wildlife photos, you would probably need a camera that has interchangeable lenses.) Once you have determined your needs, visit a large camera store and talk to a salesperson. There are many brands on the market, at many prices and the salesperson will help you determine which is the best one for you.

How to Submit Transparencies

Q. *Should Ektachrome (or other) transparencies be mounted, i.e., in the form of slides, when submitted to markets? And should they be enclosed in any special holder, or is a standard #10 envelope acceptable?*

A. No, there aren't any standard procedures for submitting Ektachrome transparencies to prospective magazines. Many editors, however, do prefer the 8x10 plastic holders in which Ektachrome transparencies can be slipped since this allows viewing of a quantity at the same time and protects the transparencies.

Copyright

Q. *A magazine is using a photo of mine (along with article) which I would like to copyright. Never before have I used a photo which I thought I wanted to protect, so I'm not sure how to go about this.*

A. If you wanted to copyright a photograph of yours you would have to advise the editor in advance so he could publish the copyright symbol alongside the photo with your name as the copyright owner. You would also have to write for the necessary copyright forms from the Register of Copyright, Library of Congress, Washington, D.C. 20559, fill them out and return with the $10 copyright fee, and two copies of the published photo.

Copyrighting Unpublished Photos

Q. *Is there any advantage in registering for copyright an unpublished photo? I have several photos that are "different" and I know I can sell them. The Copyright Office has told me that after I have filed and received my photo copyright certificate, I must pay another $10 fee once the photo is bought and henceforth published in a magazine. Now I'm not rich and this would amount to $20 in fees. I believe it'd be best to submit the photo with "one-time rights only" to the magazine and after it's published, copyright it myself.*

A. The only advantage I can think of for going to the extra expense of copyrighting an unpublished photo is if you think it might be sold to a client who would use it in an uncopyrighted publication or use it as part of, say, a TV commercial that they didn't copyright. If you think you'll be selling to a copyrighted magazine and still want the copyright in your name (not the magazine's) you'd have to get a separate copyright for yourself for this photo and the notice would have to appear with the picture. You'd have to notify the editor who accepts it that you will be applying for the separate copyright so he'll know to print "Copyright (year), (your name)" under the picture.

Model Releases

Q. *What information can you give me about necessary "releases" on subjects appearing in photos? I want to branch out into some outdoor articles, but will undoubtedly have fishing companions and guides in my photos so will need releases, etc.*

A. A sample model's release appears in *Photographer's Market* (Writer's Digest Books). This book also lists more than 1,600 places where photographers can sell their work.

Photo Pay

Q. *Are photos that have not been shot by the author, such as government photos or stock photos, purchasable by the editor when included with a manuscript? If photos are considered part of the purchase price, does the editor have to pay to use them? If so, who receives payment ... the agency where you obtained photos, the photographer who took the pictures, or the writer who submitted them?*

A. If you obtain some photos free from the government and submit them to an editor, whether the editor wants to pay for them or not varies from magazine to magazine. If the magazine does decide to pay for them, they would include payment in the purchase price to the writer.

Picture Problems

Q. *I might have the chance to interview some celebrities this summer. I cannot take the pictures, but there is a good professional photographer in this city who can. He is a complete stranger to me. Should I contact him before I query an editor or should I get the writing assignment first? If the editor does not purchase the story and pictures separately, what percentage does the photographer usually get?*

A. Before you query the editor, explain your project to the photographer and see if he would be willing and available to furnish his services this summer. Reach an agreement with him regarding payment. (Being a professional, he will let you know his usual fees.) Then in your query to the editor, you can have the added advantage of informing him that you will be able to furnish professionally taken photos of the interviewees.

Photo Details

Q. *Could you explain the difference between 2¼x2¼ and 4x5 transparencies?*

A. Both refer to the size film used in the camera. Reflex cameras like the Rolleiflex, Yashica, etc., produce negatives, or transparencies that measure 2¼x2¼ inches. The Speed Graphic and Linhof, on the other hand, can produce negatives that are 4x5 inches. The 2¼films are on rolls (size 120, 620, etc.) while the 4x5 is cut sheet film.

Photo Alterations?

Q. *In a case where one of the branches of the military's promotional and public relations department sends a news release with illustrating photo to the news media, is it OK for newspapers to use one section of that photo (masking part of the persons) to illustrate a different news item?*

A. It would be advisable for the newspaper to check with the military PR department on the use of that photo for a purpose other than was originally intended.

Photojournalist in Advertising

Q. *How does a photographer go about breaking into the advertising business? Do the big companies that have page ads in the larger magazines give assignments or do they maintain a staff?*

A. The big companies usually are clients of advertising agencies who offer photography as a regular service to the advertising agencies. A photographer who wants to break into advertising would be wise to cultivate a contact at such an agency by showing samples of his professional work comparable to what the agency is already using.

Photo Return

Q. *Can I expect to have unused photos returned to me that are not used with an article? How can I indicate that I would like to have the unused ones returned? When they are not used, these photographs belong to whom?*

A. The unused photos belong to you and you are justified in requesting their return. Enclose SASE with your submission and ask in your cover letter that unused photos be returned.

12. Writing Fiction

Adult Fiction?

Q. *Could you please define adult fiction?*

A. Adult fiction simply means that the characters, their problems and experiences, and the style of writing are intended for mature readers rather than children and teenagers.

Story Titles

Q. *In submitting short fiction to general slick magazines, what is the best procedure to follow when a good title does not come to mind? Is it better to submit an untitled story or to submit a title that does not satisfy the author? In these circumstances, should a letter accompany the piece explaining that a title is lacking and the author would like the story titled by the magazine, or that the author feels the title submitted is unsatisfactory?*

A. Titles are often subject to change by the magazines; therefore don't spend too much time worrying about them. For purposes of identification, it *is* advisable for a manuscript to have a title, so choose a simple one rather than none at all. Do not enclose any explanatory letters.

Definitions, Please

Q. *Fiction requirements of many magazines specify either "no contrived" or "no slick" stories. So far as I can determine, "contrived" means planned (what story isn't planned?) and "slick" means a slick paper (many types of stories are on slick paper). Could you please give me your definition of these terms?*

A. By "contrived," editors usually mean plots whose action is constructed in an artificial, implausible way. For example, if a character purposely sets fire to a barn to kill the man inside, that's a credible, well-motivated act. But if a fire happens to break out in the barn for no reason other than the obvious one of helping the author dispose of the man inside, that's contrived. "Slick" *did* originally refer only to the type of paper used in a magazine. But nowadays, it has come to mean the familiar, formula-type story, e.g., boys meets girl—loses girl —gets girl, which has a neat, pat (and usually happy) ending.

Problem With Heirs?

Q. *I know of no living relatives belonging to the real-life character I am basing my short story on. Am I free to continue my short fiction without thought of his living heirs?*

A. Go ahead and write your story, being careful to write nothing that could conceivably make you the victim of a lawsuit, should any of his heirs be extant and recognize him in your story. Since heirs can sue for invasion of privacy as well as libel, many writers feel safer changing names, dates, places, etc.

Children's Stories

Q. *I would like to specialize in writing for children but I need some basic instruction in how to go about this. What do you suggest?*

A. *Writing for Children and Teen-agers,* by Lee Wyndham (Writer's Digest Books) is a good basic reference in this field. You'll find detailed chapters on how to get ideas, how to handle characterization, dialog, plotting, motivation, conflict, suspense—and then how to sell it after you write it.

Rule Breakers

Q. *Maugham and Hemingway were both considered great writers. But most of their short stories did not have plots, that is "conflict." If either writer were alive today, would his stuff sell?*

A. Works that have become classics have the ability to go beyond the narrow time in which they were produced because of the universal truths and insights they offer. The stories of these writers do sell today because of their authors' inherent skill in bringing characters to life and making their problems interesting. Their work does indeed deal with the conflicts of man's relation to man and to himself.

Settings are Scenes

Q. *How does one go about isolating a scene, in dissecting a short story? To me the scenes seem somewhat continuous. I fail to see any sharp dividing line in a taut story.*

A. Whenever the action moves to a different setting, that's automatically a new scene. If, for example, a story opens in a young couple's kitchen and then moves to an incident in the husband's office, these two different settings constitute two different scenes. But suppose the story is a taut short-short in which all the action takes place in the kitchen. Then we look for a division that is not geographical but a time change. This could develop if your first scene shows the husband and wife in the kitchen at breakfast time. Then after setting this stage, you may want to have a time break to five o'clock when the wife is preparing dinner. This is a device used often. For example, "Jim stomped out during breakfast without finishing his coffee. As Ellen prepared dinner, she thought of the silly argument they had had early that day."

Fiction Query?

Q. *What should the fiction writer put in his query? Should the smaller, less well-known publications be queried at all? What should be the length?*

A. Because of the nature of fiction, editors rarely if ever expect to be queried about it. Good fiction usually defies the type of summarization or highlighting used in query letters because so many of the integral elements, e.g., style, mood, characterization, etc., would be lost. Therefore, to consider fiction fairly, most editors prefer to receive the manuscript. Also see Chapter 6.

One Part to Two Parts?

Q. *After I have sold a short-short story, can I take the story and expand it into a two- or three-part story and sell it again?*

A. The answer to this would depend on what rights you offered for sale along with your story. If the magazine you sold your story to bought only the usual First North American Serial Rights, then this means that after its appearance in this magazine just this one time, all rights to the story reverted to you. You would then be free to do what you wished with it. Simply write a letter to the purchaser of your story, asking about the rights involved in this transaction. It would be ethical to tell whomever you're going to sell subsequent versions of the story, of the story's original sales record.

Famous Name?

Q. *At what time is it permissible to use the name of a famous person in a short story? If the name was not used in an unfavorable manner, would there be any objections?*

A. Provided there are no derogatory connotations, it is permissible to use a famous person's name in a short story.

Nonformula Story

Q. *How do I write the story that is not the "formula" story? ... Every story has its beginning, middle and its ending. When studying a story an editor has called the "no formula" story, I cannot see any difference from that which is called the "formula" story ... except for the opening of that story. Setting the scene is generally used as the opening for any good story, but a story that is not considered "formula" seems to open without the setting of a scene or background. Is this the only difference or have I failed to receive the message?*

A. The message you're getting is a little garbled. While the opening of a story sometimes is a clue as to whether or not it is a "formula" story, *that* is not one of the significant differences between "formula" and "nonformula" fiction. When editors speak of the formula story, they usually mean a familiar theme treated in a predictable or familiar plot structure. Thus, the formula for the slick love story might be: boy meets girl, boy loses girl, boy gets girl. The editor who is looking for a nonformula story wants to get away from such plot situations and development. He wants an unusual central problem treated in an original manner. Very likely characterization in the story will be more important than the situation.

Young Author

Q. *I have a boxful of short stories, ranging in length from eight to 110 handwritten pages. Since I'm only 14, I wonder if there's any market you could suggest for my work or am I too young? Too, must all submitted manuscripts be typed? I find it most impossible to sit down at a typewriter and express myself.*

A. You are never too young to submit your work to markets, provided it is salable. But before you do, read and become familiar with the magazines for which you'd like to write. There are many young people's publications, and you'll find them listed in WRITER'S MARKET. Try to decide what age group would be most interested in your stories and then study any large newsstand to learn about the magazines that are geared to this readership group. Yes, manuscripts must be typed. However, there's no reason why you can't initially "express yourself" in longhand and then type up the manuscript for submission to markets.

Short Story Prize

Q. *I am writing a novel and I need to know in connection with the plot, what are the well known prizes for short stories, similar, say, to the Pulitzer Prize or Nobel Prize.*

A. There are no prizes for individual short stories comparable to the Nobel for the novel. A Pulitzer Prize in fiction might be given for a collection of short stories by a single author. Other awards given to short stories are those which are included each year in the two volumes of *Best Short Stories of the Year.* One of these is called *Prize Stories 19—: The O'Henry Awards.* The other is called *The Best American Short Stories of 19—,* etc. See also the chapter, Contests and Awards in WRITER'S MARKET.

Fact Into Fiction

Q. *What rules pertain to fictionalizing an actual event about which there was considerable mystery and secrecy? The event was a semi-scientific experiment which was unique and which received nation-wide publicity when it occurred. Since the event was unique and widely publicized, the event and all its participants would be easily recognized. Because military security is still in effect about the ex-periment, I am sure there is no possibility of doing a factual piece on the subject. Where and how is the line drawn between fact and fiction in such a case? To what degree would the event and characters have to be changed to make them fictitious?*

A. Since the event received such widespread publicity, you may use a similar idea in a fiction plot, but you would be wise to surround it with a new, invented set of characters, (e.g., one character could be made considerably younger than the real-life one, and given different personal traits and appearance), and sufficiently altered circumstances (perhaps in a different locale) so that the resultant story will be the product of your own creativity rather than just straight reporting.

More True-Life Problems

Q. *My short story embraces a particular true event in a 19th century man's life which is recorded in newspapers and books. Can I properly call it fiction even though two-thirds of the story is my own dialog and events? I wish to be fair.*

A. Yes, it is certainly permissible to fictionalize a historical event. Since you are creating the dialog and much of the dramatic action, it can properly be called fiction.

Use Real Names?

Q. *In a juvenile fiction story based on true historical incidents, may I use authentic names of teachers, mayors, ministers, businessmen, etc.?*

A. If there is nothing derogatory in your references to these people, there should be no objection to your use of their names.

13. What is Style?

Personal Style

Q. *I recently read an article by a well known fiction writer who said it was not good to read other fiction writers. He stated it would confuse his style and it may make his work seem inferior to the other writers. What is the majority's opinion on this matter?*

A. The narrow view of that particular writer is not generally shared by most writers who have one love in common—the love of reading. If reading the work of others confuses a writer's style, then such a style was probably not individual enough or rooted deeply enough to begin with. The novice writer may go through several phases of stylistic expression before he finds the one that is himself. Remember that a writer who reads only himself may find that he is writing only for himself too.

A Question on Style

Q. *I am puzzled by the idea of style. Also I would appreciate a list of the various types of style, so that I can make a study of them.*

A. Every writer has his own style because style is simply the way an author expresses his ideas. Faulkner's style, for example, is recognizably different from Hemingway's. It would be impossible to list all the various styles because of the diversity of the individuals producing them. The best way to study authors' styles is to read their works. For additional help in improving your own style, see *The Elements of Style,* by Strunk & White, (Macmillan).

First Person Always True?

Q. *How can a humorous book written in the first person (such as those by Erma Bombeck) be thought of as fiction, even allowing for exaggerated anecdotes?*

A. While probably inspired by factual bits and pieces in the writer's life, essentially these books are more imagination than reality. Writing in first person doesn't necessarily guarantee that the material is true.

14. Editorial Taboos

Magazine Taboos

Q. *What subjects are taboo in magazines?*

A. Some magazines have no taboos, and state this in their editorial requirements in WRITER'S MARKET. Others state what their particular taboos are. For instance, you wouldn't submit an article about a plane wreck to an airlines magazine. Car magazines too sometimes specify no accidents. Many men's magazines use sexy stories; others are not markets for this type. The confession magazines are now accepting stories about racial and religious conflicts which were formerly taboo. Religious magazines have their special sets of taboos which vary from magazine to magazine. Church school papers use stories which follow the precepts of their particular religion. Some state flatly "No smoking, drinking, dancing, etc." When writing for the youngest of the juvenile set, keep the ending happy. You should write for sample copies of the magazines you plan to submit to, and study them to see just what they use. Also see Chapter 25 for more information on editorial taboos.

Teenage Smokers?

Q. *I'm writing a book. Will I hurt my chances of publication if I have a few of my teenage characters smoking cigarettes? Can I name popular brands?*

A. If smoking definitely contributes to your development of the characterizations in a realistic way, use it. It's all right to name popular brands provided no derogatory references are made to them.

Teenage Book

Q. *If my story were acceptable in every other way, do you think that a publisher of teenage books would reject it because it has: 1) a fight between two teenage members of a high school football team; 2) a college-ager who is restricted to a wheelchair because of a football injury; 3) football action that gets rough, i.e., an elbow thrown at the face, nothing worse; 4) another character getting his arm broken in practice? I need to know if these could be objectionable or if there is some other flaw to my book which has met with rejections.*

A. It is highly doubtful that any of these elements alone could be responsible for the rejection of your book manuscript. Other factors, such as style, plotting, credibility, etc., should be considered.

15. Writing and Selling Books

Multiple Queries and Submissions

Q. *I have written chapters for two nonfiction books. I have sent the sample chapters and a query letter to publishers for consideration. As you well know, it can take three to four months for a publisher to analyze the market and reply to the query. Both these potential books, however, are topical. If each publisher takes that long to reply, the material I have researched and collected will become outdated. In such a case, can I send sample chapters and queries for a book to more than one editor for consideration? If not, do you have any suggestions to speed up the process?*

A. In some cases, and especially when the topic of the book is timely, it is necessary to query several firms at one time. If you send multiple queries without advising the potential publisher, though, you might have problems. For example, how would you handle the situation if you received a positive response from more than one firm? You would have to tell one of the publishers the book is being considered by another firm, which may cause that publisher to avoid any of your future book ideas. If you feel multiple submissions are necessary for your book, be sure to tell the editor what you are doing.

Book Contract

Q. *I'm writing a book, and don't know the first thing about a contract. Where can I learn more or possibly see a copy of a book contract?*

A. SASE to Writer's Digest for a free reprint of an article titled "What the Writer Should Look for in His First Book Contract," written by Irwin Karp, which appeared in an earlier issue of *Writer's Yearbook*. You can also buy a sample contract from the Society of Authors' Representatives, 101 Park Ave., New York City 10017, for 75¢, which includes postage. (Enclose stamps or coins; send no check.)

Query a Book Publisher?

Q. *Is it permissible to write a book company regarding the status of a novel? I sent a manuscript a month ago, and so far have heard nothing. Also, would you explain about sample chapters and outlines?*

A. It's permissible, but you're too impatient. It sometimes takes over three months for a publisher to report on a book-length manuscript. You'd get faster service on an outline, two or three sample chapters and a short cover letter asking if the publisher is interested in seeing more. The outline should be brief, about a page or two, depending on how long it takes to summarize the main incidents of the story.

Book Illustrator

Q. *I have a manuscript for a children's book, a fantasy, but need someone to illustrate it. It would be on a 50/50 basis and quite a few line drawings would be needed. How would you suggest I contact that sort of person?*

A. Concentrate on selling your story to a book publisher and then let *him* worry about the illustrations. He prefers to do this anyway, since he is familiar with the various styles and abilities of different illustrators, and can select the one whose talents would be most appropriate for your subject matter and for the format he wishes to use.

Publishing Your Own Book

Q. *If I have a book published or print it on my own with a mimeo machine, have it copyrighted, advertise and sell a few copies of it, will I at any time be able to offer this same book to a larger publisher, or do you think this would ruin my chances of selling it to a larger firm?*

A. Before printing this book on your own, first see if any "larger publisher" would be interested in it. Private printing could lessen established publishers' interest in a work since some prefer to be the first to present and distribute the manuscript in book form.

Nonfiction Book

Q. *I have written a self-help psychology book. It is written like a test in order to pique the reader's mind; but is also in regular manuscript form in some places. I would like to know whether I should send it to a publisher straight off, send a query, or submit it through an agent? As I am 21 and this is my first book, should I get it notarized? Should a manuscript be sent by registered mail? Could you suggest some suitable publishers?*

A. Query the publisher first and then if he expresses interest, you can submit the completed manuscript. In your letter, you might include excerpts from one of the tests and from the standard prose passages, too, so that the publisher can get an idea of your style and treatment. Notarization is not necessary. If you keep a carbon copy of your manuscript, you don't really need to send it by costly registered mail. Consult WRITER'S MARKET for the names and addresses of book publishers who indicate they are interested in self-help books.

Book Award

Q. *Could you give me any information on the Newbery and Caldecott Awards? How do you get a book nominated?*

A. These awards are given annually through the American Library Association by a member committee of children's and school librarians. Usually in November, members of the Children's Library Association receive blanks for nominating their choices for the Awards. The Newbery Medal is awarded to an author, while the Caldecott Medal goes to an illustrator of a children's book.

Book Synopsis and Outline

Q. *Should a synopsis be overall or abbreviated chapter by chapter content? How extensive should an outline be?*

A. A synopsis should provide a comprehensive summary of the contents in about two typewritten pages. An outline could cover chapter by chapter highlights.

Chapters and Synopsis?

Q. *Is it in order to send the first few chapters of a novel to a publisher, with a synopsis of the rest of the novel?*

A. Yes, as a matter of fact, many publishers prefer a synopsis, sample chapters, and cover letter rather than the complete novel manuscript. (This saves postage and wear and tear on the manuscript.)

Book Publishing Costs

Q. *When having a book published, will the author be required to furnish a large sum of money before the book will be published? If you have b&w photos you want in the book, will these cost extra?*

A. Only if the book is to be published by a subsidy publisher will the author have to foot the bill. Trade publishers assume all regular production costs. Photos usually do increase the cost of publishing a book, and here again, the publisher involved will determine who absorbs this extra expense.

Book Forewords

Q. *I can write a good introduction for my book, but because of the theme (importance of proper care in the rapid recovery of mentally ill patients), don't you think it would hold more weight if a psychiatrist wrote the introduction?*

A. Yes, an introduction by a psychiatrist would lend more authority to your book. However, this is usually handled by the publisher. In your covering letter, indicate that you know of several prominent psychiatrists who would be willing to write an introduction if the publisher is interested in the book.

Book of Short Stories

Q. *Do book publishers put out collections of short novels and stories that haven't previously been published?*

A. Yes, but rarely. More often they prefer their collections to be a combination of both published and new stories. For example, in John O'Hara's *Assembly* only ten of the 26 stories and short novels originally appeared in magazines. In the case of an unknown writer, however, the publisher is usually reluctant to bring out a collection of work that has not stood the test of print. It is easier for the beginning writer to establish his reputation through periodicals, and then try to get a book publisher interested.

Illustrating Books

Q. *I am interested in illustrating children's books, but have been unsuccessful in locating any information on the subject. Can you supply me with the information I need? I would like the size of illustrations, medium in which the work should be done, what material should the illustrations be on, etc. Are there any helpful books on the market?*

A. The publisher usually decides exactly what type of illustrations he wants for a particular book. Most publishers of children's books are well acquainted with established local illustrators and will choose the one whose talents are best suited to the specific work at hand. These publishers advise that the artist build experience as a commercial artist with an advertising agency or a printer to learn the graphic art side of preparing illustrations for reproduction, before attempting to enter the children's book field. Illustrations in color are made through the highly technical process of color separations, and the illustrator is expected to have knowledge of this process. The artist should also know the effect of certain book papers on his final artwork; he should be able to work in proportion and follow the publisher's directions for sizes. Once this experience is gained, the artist may then make up a portfolio of his best work, which should include a few things in line, some in two colors, some in full color and in a variety of media. He should then try to get an appointment with a good art director or editor in a juvenile publishing house. Often one of the best ways for the artist to get started in the juvenile field is by having an agent represent him. (See "Artists' Agents" in the Yellow Pages of the Manhattan Telephone Directory.) An agent is constantly calling on various publishers and knows what type of work they're looking for. He is in a position to recommend whichever of his clients he thinks is best equipped to handle a particular job. Most publishers work strictly on assignment, not speculation. The matter of the size of illustrations, medium, subject matter, etc. for a certain book, would have to be discussed between the publisher and the artist he selects for the assignment. Unsolicited artwork is generally considered a nuisance by the busy publisher and his editors. They also look with disfavor on the book manuscript that arrives with amateurish illustrations done by the author's friend. Authors should allow the publisher to select the illustrator. The novice illustrator is also advised to get into the habit of looking at children's books in the library, especially the Caldecott winners. As you can see, this field requires a good deal of specialized knowledge and experience. But remember, too, that publishers are always searching for a fresh new treatment of color and line drawings that say a good deal with just a few strokes of the pen. For other markets for illustrators, see *Artist's Market* (Writer's Digest Books).

Standard Royalty

Q. *Can a writer who has never had a book published (but who has sold four stories) get more than ten percent royalties? Is ten percent the "usual royalty payment"? How can I insure maximum advances? Can I do better with an agent, both royalty and advance-wise? Can you recommend agents who have been successful with "nonfiction" biographical books and who have been successful in selling them for maximum sums to the movies? The woman about whom I'm writing worked under a name that is not too euphonious. Would you advise me not to use that name? I was planning to use four of the real names of the people who helped her. I have only good things to say about these people. If I use real names, do I have to get permission from these people or permission from their heirs?*

A. Ten percent is the usual royalty payment. In order to get the best possible deal as far as royalty and an advance are concerned, it might be advisable to allow an agent to handle the contract negotiations. See Author's Agents in the latest edition of WRITER'S MARKET. You will find that in addition to providing names and addresses, this list also indicates areas, such as fiction or nonfiction, in which certain agencies specialize. If the subject of your biography is still alive, check with her on the name she would prefer to have used in the book. But in any case, the euphonious quality of a name should certainly not be a deciding factor in its usage in a nonfiction work. To be on the safe side, get permission wherever possible for the use of those people's real names.

Book Contract

Q. *Does the royalty publisher's clause (on copyright) state that the publisher shall obtain the copyright but that said copyright shall be in the name of the author and shall be that author's property? Where might I obtain an agreement contract from a royalty publisher for observation?*

A. Most royalty contracts do set up an agreement whereby the publisher takes out the copyright in the name of the author and assigns it to him. If you glance through a sampling of current bestsellers, you'll find that it is the author's name that usually follows the copyright mark. Publishers don't make a practice of sending out sample contracts for study, but you could always verify this point on any contract offered to you before you sign it.

Commercial vs. Subsidy

Q. *I have a collection of short pieces, many of which have been purchased and published by periodicals. I plan to offer these for publication in book form and have received letters of release from the periodicals. My question is, if the cost of publishing is borne by the author, can the author own the copyright, or if it is published on a royalty basis, can the author own the copyright?*

A. All books published by standard royalty book publishers are copyrighted in the name of the author. Even if the author pays to have the book published through a subsidy publisher, he should require that the book be copyrighted in his name.

Book Distribution

Q. *Do you know where I might obtain a list of book distributors? I am having my book printed myself and although I have numerous helpful contacts (publicists, etc.), I want and probably need a distributor.*

A. *The American Book Trade Directory* (published by R. R. Bowker Co. and available in most libraries) contains a list of the names and addresses of the major newsstand distributors and book wholesalers whom you might contact.

Textbook Royalties

Q. *I would like to know if textbook publishers have a standard royalty schedule. Does the same standard royalty apply to textbooks as well as books in the trade division?*

A. No, textbook publishers do not have the same royalty schedule as trade book publishers. College textbooks may vary from eight to 19% of the *net* price the publisher receives, while elementary and secondary texts may be only three to five percent based on the amount of illustration cost and staff work by the publisher.

License to Sell?

Q. *I have written a book advocating that the United States should use a three-party political system. I am considering having the book (100,000) words) printed, taking out my own copyright, and distributing the book myself until it realizes a market or dies a fizzle. What kind of license, if any, will I need to sell and distribute my book? And, will you please recommend a reputable and economical printer in the Los Angeles area to handle a paperback edition?*

A. If there is any specific license you need to sell and distribute your unique book, you had best clarify this with your local city officials and also officials of your state. A list of book manufacturers appears in the directory, *Literary Market Place,* c/o R. R. Bowker, 1180 Ave. of the Americas, New York City 10036 (also available at most main branch public library reference departments).

Second Edition

Q. *I published my own book and want a second edition. I plan to send a copy to each of ten publishers. What should I shay to them?*

A. When submitting a copy of your book to ten different publishers to interest them a second edition, you should indicate that you are making a simultaneous submission of this book to a number of publishers and would appreciate a response from them as to whether or not they would be interested in publishing a second edition.

Standard Contract

Q. *What is the "standard contract" which trade book publishers offer to those whose manuscripts are accepted?*

A. The standard book contract usually offers ten percent of the retail price on the first 5,000 copies sold, 12½% on the next 5,000 copies and 15% on all over 10,000. A reprint of the article, "What the Beginner Should Know About His First Book Contract," is available from WRITER'S DIGEST. SASE for this reprint.

Free Listings?

Q. *I am in the process of publishing my own book. Please inform me as to how I can notify all libraries and how I can advertise at an inexpensive rate.*

A. If you would like to call your book to the attention of librarians, you could do so by sending a publicity release or similar newsworthy article to the various library magazines. Ask your librarian to show you some of these publications, such as *American Libraries, Library Journal,* etc. You could also write advertising managers of these publications to learn their advertising rates. The only other way to bring your book to the attention of all librarians would be to send a mailing to a list of libraries taken from the *American Library Directory.*

Subsidy Publish?

Q. *Should a new writer submit to subsidy publishing houses? Perhaps it might be of some interest to those of us who do have material we'd like to get into print, but are skeptical.*

A. Only if a commercial publisher cannot be found to publish your book and you can afford to pay to have your own book published—at a fee which may run into several thousands of dollars—should you as a new writer submit to a subsidy publishing house. If a book is good enough to be published you should send it first to a regular royalty publisher who will pay *you* rather than ask you to underwrite the cost of publishing the book. A comprehensive list of both royalty and subsidy publishers appears in WRITER'S MARKET.

Picture Books

Q. *I've written several children's stories that my children really like. I've been told that I should send them somewhere and get them published. Thanks to* Writer's Digest *I have an idea just where to send them. What I want to know is, how?*

A. Picture book manuscripts are typed double-spaced with the author's name and address in the upper left corner of the first page of the manuscript.

Copy of Contract

Q. *Where can I get a copy of the standard Authors Guild Contract?*

A. "Your Book Contract," a guide for the use of members of the Authors Guild in the negotiation of contracts with book publishers comes with your membership. Details on eligibility requirements and annual dues are available from The Authors Guild, 234 W. 44th St., New York City 10036.

Dedications?

Q. *Do book dedications accompany manuscripts when they are mailed to the publisher, or are they added after the manuscripts have been sold?*

A. Book dedications are usually submitted by the author after the book has been accepted by the publisher.

Posthumous Work

Q. *My husband, a freelance writer, died two years ago, leaving numerous stories, several novels and other material which has not been published. I would like to submit the novels to publishers as two of them came very close to acceptance. How do I go about doing this? In* *other words, must I mention the circumstances when submitting the novel?*

A. If the book is accepted by a publisher, you could then explain the situation, since the book contract would have to take into account that you are his legal heir. Don't confuse the issue until that point, however. Just submit the manuscripts for judgment on their own merits.

Rights Offered?

Q. *When submitting a book manuscript to a publisher for consideration, what data concerning "rights" should be attached?*

A. It's not necessary to discuss the matter of rights when submitting a book manuscript to a publisher. If they decide to publish the book, the contract they draw up and present to you will have all the rights provisions spelled out. If you agree with them, you can sign the contract; if you don't you can discuss it further with them before coming to terms.

Columns Into Book

Q. *I have copyrighted some printed material that I am trying to sell as columns to newspapers. If it is published in the papers and I then want to put the same material into book form, would I have any copyright problems?*

A. Although unpublished manuscripts in general cannot be copyrighted, it is possible to copyright a printed collection of columns. As long as you are selling only serial rights to the newspaper columns you have copyrighted, book rights belong to you. The best thing to do when submitting the printed column to the newspapers is to print in the upper right corner of the column, "North American Serial Rights Only," and remember that the book must acknowledge the original copyright date of the columns.

Mimeographed Book?

Q. *I am working on my first book manuscript. I have it in mind to publish my own book. It will be 80 to 100 pages. I will use letter-size paper folded, making pages about 5½x8½ inches. Has anyone ever produced a mimeographed paperback book? I know about mimeograph magazines, but I can't recall reading anything about such a book. Can I get a copyright on the mimeographed book? If, after offering it as a mimeographed work, I later wish to have it done by the printer I might choose, would there have to be another copyright?*

A. Someone probably has produced a mimeographed paperback book. As far as the Copyright Office is concerned, a mimeographed manuscript is a "published work." If you wish to have the mimeographed version redone later by a printer you could ask the Copyright Office, Library of Congress, Washington, D.C. 20559 for information on how to show your copyright on this second printing.

Promote a Cookbook

Q. *I am planning to write and publish a special cookbook. Can I advertise and sell it with a new products release?*

A. You could certainly try your luck with a new products release on your special cookbook. (I'm assuming you have received permission to use any recipes in this cookbook that are not your own.) What success you'd have would depend on how unique the cookbook was and how newsworthy the editors of these new products columns felt it was. Good luck.

Using Recipes for Cookbook

Q. *I'm writing a cookbook, and would like to use many recipes I've clipped from newspapers over the years. Since most newspapers are not copyrighted, and everything published in them is in public domain, is it permissible for me to use recipes I have from the paper?*

A. Only a very few newspapers (like the *New York Times,* for example) are copyrighted, so any recipes you got from uncopyrighted newspapers would be OK for you to use. But, you would not be at liberty to use recipes from copyrighted newspapers or magazines, as is, without infringing on the author's copyright. Many cookbook authors who don't know the sources of many recipes they've gathered over the years do these things: 1) Alter the number or quantity of individual ingredients in the recipe. 2) Completely rewrite the directions. Although ingredients themselves cannot be copyrighted, the presentation of the recipe and directions can be copyrighted. Serious cookbook authors, of course, have created many original recipes and test-cooked every item in their cookbooks. But many cookbooks are simply compiled as you're doing. If your local library has back issues of *Writer's Yearbook,* you might want to look up the article "If You Want to Write a Cookbook" which appeared in the 1972 edition. Also see WRITER'S DIGEST April 1976 issue, which includes "Serving Up a Cookbook Manuscript" and other articles and markets for cookbooks and food writing.

More Cookbook Problems

Q. *I am working on a cookbook in which I am going to use old family recipes, adapted, of course, to present day materials. I wonder if I need a release form from people from whom I secured recipes since there will be no payment made, other than a copy of the cookbook. If so, would you suggest a form to be used?*

A. Yes, it would be a good idea to get a release from each of the people from whom you are assembling recipes for your cookbook. Ask them to sign a form similar to the following: "For value received, I assign the rights to my recipe for '_____' to '_____' for use in her cookbook, '_____'." The "value received" is, of course, the copy of the cookbook you're going to give each of the contributors.

Tapes from Book

Q. *Some years ago, I wrote a children's book about the whaling era; it included several stories of foreign lands, each having a special song.*

The book was published in 1956—copyrighted in my name. The book is now out-of-print. As the stories and songs are my own material, I would like to know if I have the right to make tape recordings of them for sale to a publisher who produces visual aids and programs for school use. If there are restrictions to such usage, will you please tell me how I can meet them?

A. Unless the book contract you signed with the original publisher of your children's book about the whaling era reserved to them the right to make tape recordings of them, they are yours to use. These special rights for the use of material contained in books is usually made the subject of a special clause in the contract and you should review the contract to see whether you, or the publisher, or both, share in these rights.

Bibliography

Q. *I am writing a book which, though not a learned document, uses material from about 20 references. In all except one or two instances, I have taken no quotations from these sources. I don't wish to clutter up the book with a lot of reference symbols to indicate where I have drawn from sources. I would like to acknowledge all such unquoted references in an appendix. Can you advise me?*

A. Why not simply make a bibliography, as you suggest, to accompany your manuscript at the end, and precede it by a statement such as, "The author acknowledges the following references used in preparation of this text: ..." If your publisher prefers a different method, you can work that out between you. Where you have quoted directly, you should footnote within the text the appropriate books quoted.

Reprint Book

Q. *I paid for the printing of a small "how-to" booklet (34 pages), but don't know how to promote it. Could I send it to a publisher and expect it to be accepted, or because I printed it myself, would he refuse it?*

A. A publisher would not necessarily refuse your 34-page how-to booklet just because you printed it yourself, but rather because book publishers don't buy such short books. You'd have to try to sell it to a how-to-do-it magazine which might use it for a subscription premium or for resale to their readers. Or, you might try to sell it to some manufacturer of how-to tools or materials that might resell it or give it away to customers. An author has to be constantly searching for promotional ideas when promoting a book he's published himself.

Obtaining Permission

Q. *Is the writer of a how-to book required to obtain permission to use names and addresses in the following respects: Names and addresses of sources of equipment and supplies necessary in executing the project being explained in the book ... and ... titles of books recommended for supplementary reading, together with the authors' and publishers' names.*

A. It is not necessary to request permission for use of the titles in your bibliography, but you might wish to check with the suppliers for permission to include their names and addresses in your reference list.

Loan of Artwork

Q. *I am presently working on a comprehensive science fact book, and as a beginning writer, I have one very simple question to ask of you concerning the mechanics of assembling material for the book. Let's assume I am perusing a book written by author X, and in this book appears a graph, chart, drawing, or photograph which I would like to use in my own work. I know I must obtain permission from the author/publisher to use his materials, but how do I obtain the pertinent drawings, etc., themselves? That is, do I write to the author or publisher for a manuscript-ready print, or do I hire a draftsman to make copies from the original? Surely, reproductions from the printed book itself would be unsatisfactory—loss of clarity, detail, and so forth. What is the usual procedure here?*

A. The usual procedure would be for the publisher to decide whether to write the original publisher for loan of the camera ready art and reprint permission charges; or to write for permission and have his own art department re-do the art. It's best for the author not to do more than include Xerox copies of the art he wishes to obtain reprint permission on, before finding an actual publisher.

16. Creating the Novel

Technical Accuracy?

Q. *In writing a novel concerning the life of a professional person, such as a laboratory technician, would the author need official verification of the accuracy of technical matter in it before a book publisher would publish it, assuming the rest of the book was of publishable quality?*

A. In a cover letter, it might be helpful to state the sources on which the technical information is based. If the publisher is interested and requires further substantiation, he will let you know.

Switch Viewpoint?

Q. *In writing a novel using the major character viewpoint, is it permissible to switch—from chapter to chapter—from the third person to the first (and vice versa) or would this be too disturbing to the reader?*

A. This switching of major character viewpoint from first to third person is permissible, in the novel length, but it would probably be less distracting to readers if all the viewpoints were in the same person.

Reader Identification

Q. *I am considering a novel about a ballerina—a 14-year-old girl— and she is telling the story. I am concerned about reader identification. Will adult readers "identify" with a leading character of this age?*

A. It's rare, but adult readers *have* been known to identify with younger heroes and heroines. Shakespeare's Juliet was only about 14. Since there is presently a strong need for books geared to teenage interests, you might be wise to develop your story as juvenile fiction. With teenage girls making up most of your readers, you should have no worries about their identification with your young ballerina.

Novel Manuscript

Q. *I have just finished writing a novel. Could you tell me what the margins should be on a manuscript?*

A. The margins on the left and right sides, the top and the bottom should be at least one and one-fourth inch.

Author's Name

Q. *Does the name of the writer of a book-length manuscript have to appear on every page of the manuscript? I was under the impression that the writer's name and address were only necessary on the title page.*

A. The recommended form includes the author's name in the upper left-hand corner of each page and the page number in the upper right-hand corner. The appearance of the author's name on every page is simply a form of protection for you and a help to the editor in case some pages inadvertently get separated from the rest during reading and handling. Most publishers, incidentally, prefer pages to be numbered consecutively—not by page number within each chapter.

The Rules?

Q. *I am doing research for a proposed biographical novel, my first of this type. The famous people on whom I am basing my novel lived in the early 1800s. Naturally I am not always able to get to an original letter or document written by the subject, and so I am taking much of this from factual books of other writers in which they quote from these originals. ... Can you tell me please the rules about biographical novels? Must I get permission from all of these authors I have read in order to put certain words in my character's lips which obviously he has said? Must I get permission from whoever might have the original letters or manuscripts or documents ... if I can find whoever has them? And how about a book that was written in this 1800 period by the famed person himself ... may I use this material in building up my character? What about any living descendants of these famed people ... could they object?*

A. In a novel of this type, you could acknowledge, in an introduction or preface, the sources on which the factual material is based. Write to the book publishers, describing your project and asking their permission to use the letters they published. It isn't necessary to contact the individual authors. To be on the safe side, you might also write to the publisher of the book written by the famous character himself, requesting permission to make use of that material. As for the descendants, there is the delicate question of the "right of privacy." Since each state has its own laws about this right, consult a lawyer who could advise you how much latitude you have under law. Incidentally, a fact worth remembering is that playwright-producer Dore Schary paid $18,615 to Franklin D. Roosevelt, Jr. to compensate for "loss of privacy" caused by *Sunrise at Campobello*.

How Many Readers?

Q. *I wonder if you could give me some idea of the way a book publisher handles an unsolicited manuscript. If the first person to read the book does not like it, does the manuscript go any further or is it rejected then and there? If he thinks it has possibilities, does it then go to a second and third reader, etc.? Also, does a standard rejection slip* *without any comment usually indicate that the manuscript did not arouse any interest at all with that particular publishing house?*

A. The first reader is as anxious to find a bestseller as you are to write one. Through his experience and training he is able to spot those manuscripts that show promise and those that do not. If he feels the book has no market potential at all, he will reject it then and there. If it has possibilities, it may be passed on to another reader or to an editor. By a process of consultation and elimination the market-able manuscripts are decided upon. A standard rejection slip can mean several different things: the publisher may have just bought a similar novel, or they've already asked one of their other authors to do a similar book, or the publisher does not feel he could make money with that particular book, even though some member of his staff may have found some degree of merit in the work.

Novel, Magazine Length

Q. *When writing a novel, magazine length (25,000 words), how does one go about beginning the first page? I don't mean the actual writing; I have it written. I want to know what goes on the first page. Is it the title, the second page a list of the characters, and the third, the first page of the first chapter?*

A. The title pages should have your name and address in the upper left-hand corner. In the upper right-hand corner, state the approximate number of words, and the rights being offered for sale. Centered several spaces below that should be the title and your byline. Then about four spaces below that, center "Chapter One." Skip about three lines, and then begin your story. There is no need to list the characters.

Fiction Techniques

Q. *For the past ten years I have been very active in religious work in a rural county. I desire to write up these experiences in book form. Each chapter will represent a short story with a unifying overall story* *thread and quite a bit of local color. What effects can I use to heighten story interest?*

A. Use plenty of dialog, include vivid human-interest details, build a mood (through weather, landscape, etc.), try to create suspense by suggesting your own emotional reactions to a situation, and wherever appropriate, make a humorous observation about life in general as a result of some specific experience. Above all, keep your style lively and colorful so that readers will enjoy listening to your narrator. If you feel inhibited by the fact that your characters are actual living persons, you might have a freer hand if you fictionalize the events and make enough changes in the characters so that they become *your* literary creations, even though originally based on real people.

Time in the Novel

Q. *I have had a novel in mind for almost ten years. My insurmountable problem is one of skillfully covering too many years without taking the reader's mind like a kangaroo on a long journey. Can you advise whether to 1) cut down on the number of years covered in the novel; 2) cut down on the detail during those years; 3) cut down on both of the above; 4) lengthen the novel to include both, then return later with a more skillful knife.*

A. First you'll have to decide exactly how many years the story needs. If the same basic story can be told in either five or 15 years, by all means choose the shorter period. Remember that for dramatic purposes, you can telescope events that might, in real life, be spread over several years. Regardless of how much time the story spans, you must be discriminating in your choice of detail. Don't include anything that does not keep the action moving forward toward the climax. Avoid all irrelevancies and descriptions for description's sake. Naturally the more important incidents will be developed in full scenes. But information of minor significance can sometimes be handled by brief transitional summaries that link the highlights together. There is also the flashback that can help a story make a time leap; but this technique should be used sparingly because too much hopping back and forth between the past and the present can create havoc with readers' time sense. For additional tips on novel writing, see *One Way to Write Your Novel*, by Dick Perry and *Writing Popular Fiction*, by Dean R. Koontz, (Writer's Digest Books).

Novel Outline

Q. *In preparing an outline of a novel, just how much material should be in the outline? Would only a sentence or two, stating only the main event of the chapters be enough? Something like this: Chapter No. 5 —Helen learns that John is secretly married to her sister, Marie?*

A. The outline should be a little more detailed, suggesting scene changes and the specific action that leads to new developments (such as *how* Helen discovers this secret marriage). Remember, the outline has to be provocative enough to arouse the publisher's interest.

17. Reaping With Reprints

Resubmitting Articles

Q. *Over the years, I have contributed a great deal of material to our local natural history group's mimeographed magazine, gratis. Would it now be permissible to sell some of these articles? If so, is it necessary to tell the prospective buyer that it has been used, and the details?*

A. Since your mimeographed magazine presumably is not copyrighted, all the material it contains is in the public domain, which leaves you (or anyone else) free to make whatever use of it you wish. It would be ethical to advise prospective buyers where and when the articles first appeared. You would have to significantly rewrite these articles to now obtain copyright protection in magazines.

Selling Your Story Twice

Q. *I have sold a Christmas story. Now could I legally try to sell this same story to other juvenile publications accepting simultaneous submissions? Or does this apply only to articles? If I may do this, where is the proper place to indicate "simultaneous submissions" or "sold to so-and-so"?*

A. Multiple submissions may be made for fiction as well as non-fiction in the field of religious markets. Place a note about such submissions and/or previous sale in the upper right-hand corner of the first page of your manuscript.

Clippings

Q. *How would I obtain permission to publish items and articles that I have clipped from newspapers over a period of time? Would permission from the newspapers be enough—or would I have to go to the source, the wire services?*

A. It depends on what you're clipping and who owns the copyright. Straight news items cannot be copyrighted, so you don't need permission on those, but certain syndicated columns, features, and wire service exclusive interviews are. Write to the newspaper first, requesting permission to publish their items and they'll advise whether further correspondence is necessary. The addresses of the two major wire services are: The Associated Press, General Office, 50 Rockefeller Plaza, New York City 10020; and United Press International, General Offices, News Building, 220 E. 42 St., New York City 10017. The names and addresses of other wire services may be found in the *Editor and Publisher Year Book.*

Reselling Your Story

Q. *Would you please tell me how I would sell a story to a magazine so that I may sell to a number of magazines?*

A. The first time you sell a story, specify first serial rights only, then all secondary rights will belong to you and you can try to resell this story to another magazine that will use previously published material. You should naturally inform such subsequent magazines where and when the story originally appeared.

Serial Rights

Q. *About ten years ago, I sold a story to* Modern Romances. *There was no mention of serial rights but the check I endorsed stated they* *were buying all serial rights. Can I now sell second serial rights to another publication?*

A. Since the magazine bought all rights, the second serial rights are no longer yours to sell. You might try writing the editor to see if she will reassign the rights to you.

Prison Paper Reprint

Q. *I am an inmate of a state prison. If I sell a story to a religious magazine, can I in turn "give" it to our prison paper to print? Our prison paper is not a copyrighted paper.*

A. If the religious magazine is not copyrighted, then you may "give" the story to your paper. If the magazine is copyrighted and even buys all rights, then you'll probably be able to make some arrangement with them for the reprint of the story in your paper, but you would have to write them.

Adapt a Poem?

Q. *I feel that a certain narrative poem written in the 1800s I found in a school textbook with a 1963 copyright, could be adapted into a fine play, especially for television. Must the playwright secure permission to make such an adaptation?*

A. It would be best to check with the publisher on the copyright protection of this poem. Even though the poem was written in the last century, its present appearance might be its first publication, in which case the copyright would make permission necessary.

Resell Another Way?

Q. *An original party plan, which I recently sold to a leading children's magazine, included a novel idea for a party invitation. Do the rights purchased by the magazine prohibit me from selling the invitation to a greeting card company?*

A. If the children's magazine lists which rights it buys in WRITER'S MARKET, or indicated which rights it buys on the check you received for the plan, that is your answer. If you're not aware exactly what rights the magazine did buy, then by all means drop them a note and clarify this point before you resubmit your idea to a greeting card company. If they only bought first, or one-time serial rights, you're home free. Although ideas themselves cannot be copyrighted, the particular presentation of the idea—in this case, a party invitation—could be covered by copyright.

Resell Idea?

Q. *I recently came across an old story of mine published in a senior high magazine. It seemed quite good and I think with a little updating and a slightly different twist at the end it would be suitable for a young person's magazine. Would there be any reason I could not do this?*

A. Since you do intend to revise the published story (which is in the public domain if the high school magazine was not copyrighted), it would be all right to market it as a new work for current magazines.

Weekly Articles

Q. *Recently I wrote several articles for a small, semimonthly, rural area newspaper. As I received no compensation, must I get a release from the publisher if I wish to submit a slightly revised version to nationally-known magazines?*

A. Since there was no exchange of money, there was probably also no statement by the publisher that he wanted further rights to any of the material he obtained from you. Check with the publisher to see what rights he obtained.

Pre-Ann Landers?

Q. *Just recently, while cleaning out a very old writing desk, I came across a section of an old newspaper, which is nearly 50 years old.*

While scanning the question and answer column, such as we have today like Ann Landers and Dear Abby, I found to my great amusement, some of the funniest questions and answers I have seen in a long time. Most of the questions dealt with dresses, hair styles and questions like "Am I of the right size?" Here some sizes were given, such as 42-27-37, plus the weight and height. I would like to submit these for sale, but know of no outlet for them. Would you please advise me on how these should be typed and also where I could send them.

A. If the Question and Answer Section of the old newspaper was copyrighted, as are Ann Landers and Dear Abby today, you would not be free to use this material. Since, if the copyright were renewed it would be valid for 56 years (or more, if it expired since 1962) you would have to take this into consideration. If the column was not copyrighted, you would be free to submit this material to filler markets which might be interested in the subject matter. WRITER'S MARKET lists numerous magazines and tells what kinds of filler material they buy. These filler items should be typed one to a page with your name and address in the upper left-hand corner, the date and source of the item beneath the item and the manuscript accompanied by a SASE.

Book Reprints

Q. *I would like to know what a book publisher means when he says he publishes reprints. Standard contract offers are made for reprints. How does one submit reprint books to a publisher for consideration?*

A. If you have published a hardcover book, its sales have run their course, and you think it still has potential sale in paperback, you could write a query to a reprint publisher describing your book, providing details on the date and publisher of the original version and asking if he'd like to see the book for possible reprinting. Most reprinting is done in paperback, from books originally published in hardcover. Sometimes, however, it works the other way. Some publishers of reprints are firms which take historical works and/or other books which are no longer under copyright and reprint them with new material added.

Re-use Without Permission?

Q. *For several years, in addition to my freelance writing, I have edited a monthly bulletin for a club of which I am a member. I have recently been thinking of gathering all my bulletin material and publishing it in a small book. Each issue of the bulletin is published with the sentence, "Permission to reprint material from this bulletin is granted provided proper credit is given." May I legally gather and print my material without permission from the club? I intend to make it very clear that the material came from the bulletin.*

A. Your safest bet would be to clarify with the club that you plan to reprint material which you originally edited in their monthly bulletin. It will probably save you headaches later if you clear this with everybody first. You will be pointing out, of course, that the bulletin will be credited, and that's their main concern, but it's best to tell them first.

Story into Book?

Q. *If a children's story has been accepted and published in a magazine, is it possible to gain permission to offer it to a book publisher for publication as a picture book? If so, what procedure should be followed?*

A. Yes, a published story can be turned into book form provided the author has retained the book rights. You will need to check with the magazine to ascertain which rights were purchased along with the story. If they bought *all* rights, then you'll have to try to make some special arrangement concerning the book rights. If, on the other hand, you own these rights, submit your story to the book publisher and be sure to inform him of its previous publication.

Revise and Sell Publicity Features?

Q. *As a publicist I write and send feature stories to newspapers which frequently use the material verbatim. If I should select a better than* *average piece, delete the commercial overtones and send the story to a magazine, where do I stand legally and ethically?*

A. There is no reason you couldn't resell revised versions of feature articles to magazines you wrote originally as a publicist and placed in local newspapers. Although you remove the commercial overtones, the company's industry in general would probably benefit from the national coverage.

Poetry Resubmitted

Q. *About 20 years ago, I had a book of poetry published. Can I now send these poems around to markets, and should the book be mentioned? I also write two columns for free. Should these be copyrighted?*

A. If you own the serial rights to your book of poems, you are free to try to sell them to magazines that do use reprints; but you should mention the book in which they originally appeared. If your columns appear in an uncopyrighted publication, and you don't want them to fall into public domain, then you should see to it that they are accompanied by a notice of copyright in your name. Write to Register of Copyrights, Library of Congress, Washington D.C. 20559 for the proper form.

American Resale?

Q. *I have sold some verses and articles to a British magazine and would like to try to sell them to American publications also. Can I still offer first North American rights? Should I make mention of the fact that they have already been printed in Britain?*

A. It would be fair to advise the American publications of the British sales record of your material. You would also need to check with the British magazine which bought your work to find out what rights, if any, they still retain to this material.

Story Rewrite

Q. *Two years ago a short story of mine appeared in my high school's literary magazine which is published annually by the school and contains work submitted by students only. Recently I have added more to the story and changed some of the beginning, but the majority of what appeared in the magazine is still the same. I would like to know if this work is considered a published manuscript. I would like to try to sell it, but most magazines want short stories not previously published.*

A. Yes, your work has been "published"; but since the school magazine probably wasn't copyrighted, and since you have revised the story, thereby technically producing a new work, you are free to try marketing the *new* version as an unpublished manuscript. ("Publication" in an uncopyrighted magazine places 'that' version of your work in the public domain.)

Multiple Sales?

Q. *Recently a photographer asked me to write copy to go with his pictures. To date we have completed two Sunday pictorial articles. Now he wants to resubmit these sold articles to subsequent markets. Can we keep reselling them to different newspapers and magazines?*

A. You will have to check on what rights were bought by the original Sunday pictorial. And, of course, resales should be to noncompeting magazines and newspapers.

18. Filling in With Fillers

What Are Fillers?

Q. *Describe fillers to me. How many different kinds of fillers are there?*

A. Filler material can be jokes, anecdotes, definitions, one-liners, puns, etc. Or it can be humor found in already published material—such as typos or printer's errors. Puzzles, quizzes, and word games are also used as fillers. Household, sewing and cooking tips might be used as fillers for some magazines. Finally, there are newspaper clippings of short news items which constitute probably the largest editorial use of filler space. Newspaper clippings, though, should be directly related to the publication's editorial content.

Getting Started

Q. *I've thought about submitting fillers, but how do I get started?*

A. A filler can be just about anything you choose to make it as long as it's informative or entertaining, or both. Read plenty of magazines. Know what type of material a magazine offers the readers—get the feel of its content and its worth as a possible market. Study the markets listed in WRITER'S MARKET—especially in the paragraph that gives information on fillers and requirements for same. And read at least one book on filler writing before you try your hand at it. When submitting fillers, type only one to a page; or if it is a newspaper clipping, paste it on an 8½x11 sheet of white paper and type below it the issue date and name of the newspaper from which it was clipped. In either case, of course, your name and address goes in the upper left-hand corner.

Multiple Submissions

Q. *Is it permissible to send the same filler item to more than one publication at the same time?*

A. Yes, you can do that, but use some judgment in submitting to multiple markets. Try not to overlap markets that have the same audiences, for example.

One At a Time?

Q. *For selling filler items, is it wiser to send in one item at a time in either letter form or on a postcard? Do editors object to getting such items from writers trying to make money?*

A. It's all right to submit several filler items at one time. But each should be double-spaced on a separate full-size sheet of paper. If the material is suitable for an editor's needs, he'll be happy to be helping along a struggling writer.

Fillers to Resell

Q. *I recently bought some bound volumes of old magazines ... The Youth's Companion (dating from 1897 through 1908). There are many perfectly delightful human interest fillers. How could I best use them ... If I could use them at all? Could I rewrite and bring them up to date to fit our more "modern" humor?*

A. Since these fillers are now in the public domain, you may indeed use them however you wish. You could modernize them and try to sell them individually, or as part of a collective article.

Resubmitting Fillers

Q. *When is the writer safe in resubmitting fillers to other magazines after not receiving an acknowledgment or a return of his material from the first magazine he tried?*

A. Unless the magazine gives a specific reporting time, you should feel free to resubmit if two months go by without a word.

Re-use Fillers?

Q. *As a beginning writer I am considering submitting some children's sayings and anecdotes as fillers in an effort to earn expenses while getting started in the writing field. My question is, will it be ethical to use any of these that might be sold for publication in longer articles at a later date or will I no longer be free to use them at all? Some of them are personal experiences.*

A. Whether you could use the children's sayings you are planning to submit as fillers in longer articles at a later date, would depend on what rights are bought by the magazine publishing them. If they bought all rights, you may have problems. (Jokes, for example, cannot be copyrighted but whether "children's sayings" would be so considered by the courts is unknown.) If they only bought first rights to the material, then you would, of course, be free to use the material elsewhere again.

Submitting Fillers

Q. *When sending epigrams, gags, etc. to magazines, is it "professional" to send them on 8½x11 sheets—or can you send them on index-size cards? Should you put your name, address and word count on the top as you do for large material? What about a covering letter?*

A. The sheet is preferable to the index card, and your name and address should be included in standard manuscript form. A covering letter is not necessary.

Fillers

Q. *Some authors rewrite unusual news stories to submit to other markets. Are there laws against using and reusing ideas culled from newspapers? Does this apply to bylined features as well?*

A. While news items are facts open to anyone's interpretation, feature articles usually have a specific angle or slant, and involve the research, selectivity and interpretations of the individual writer. These are protected by the overall copyright on the paper, if there is one; or by the syndicate if it is a syndicated feature.

Using Quips

Q. *If a filler writer publishes a one- or two-line quip, is it considered fair for another writer to copy it verbatim, changing only one word, and passing it off as his own? I'm asking this because I've run across such cases and am wondering.*

A. No. He should indicate the original source when resubmitting elsewhere. Jokes, however, cannot be copyrighted, so they're actually in the public domain.

19. Working With a Collaborator

Pay for Life Story?

Q. *A friend has offered to relate to me the very unusual story of her life, for use in a novel. The entire writing job will be mine, as well as marketing, etc. I feel she is entitled to some percentage of any profit from the novel. What is the usual percentage in such cases? Am I within my rights to request exclusive use of the material at any later date to use other than for the novel in question?*

A. In cases of this type, as well as in biographies, the subject whose life is being used is not usually given any payment except the satisfaction of seeing his life story in print. If you feel a personal obligation, why not simply offer a flat sum (whatever is agreeable to both parties) for use of this material, dependent, of course, on its sale to a publisher. If at all possible, you should secure legal help with any financial arrangement that is made. Since there are others who are probably familiar with the events of your subject's life, you cannot reasonably expect to have exclusive control over this material. Remember that "facts" themselves cannot be copyrighted, although your presentation of them in books, articles, etc. can be copyrighted.

Collaboration Arrangements

Q. *An acquaintance has asked me to collaborate in the preparation and marketing of material in the nontechnical category. Enough material has been assembled for about 120,000 words, but it is in rough* *draft form and will need to be rewritten for submission to a publisher. My acquaintance has no knowledge of the mechanics involved so that every bit of the work will be up to me to do. How do I go about being completely fair with her? What agreement should there be regarding money—both profit and preliminary expenses?*

A. Collaboration arrangements naturally vary according to the situations and individuals involved. Some collaborators work on a 50-50 basis all the way down the line. You imply that you will be doing most of the work from here on in, so you may feel entitled to a larger percentage, say 60-40, if that is agreeable to the lady. Another alternative might be to agree on a flat sum for your help in preparing the material for submission to a publisher, plus a percentage of the royalties in case of sale. Discuss the matter frankly with your collaborator and if possible, obtain some legal advice that would protect both your rights in this situation.

Friendly Arrangements

Q. *I have been offered the opportunity of collaborating on some stories. A friend of mine went on safari to Africa and took some excellent photographs of his hunting trips. He wants me to write his experiences and he will furnish the photos. If the stories are sold, what percentage do I pay him? Of course all money received for photos would be his, but I have no idea how much I should share with him of the money received for a story.*

A. If you are successful in selling some articles to sport and outdoor magazines for example, and the photographer is paid separately for his photographs, you should receive the entire amount of money for the work you put into the article. There is no set rule of thumb for collaboration fees between writers and photographers. They have to decide when the item is sold how much each person contributed to the sale and make their share of the check reflect that. If the magazine pays the photographer and writer separately, you are relieved of making this decision yourself, since the magazine editor is deciding what proportion of the total check he feels is due each partner.

Collaborating With The Expert

Q. *When a writer and an expert in a field collaborate on an article, how are fees received usually divided? I am thinking especially of a situation in which the expert directs the writer to sources of information and reads copy for factual accuracy as his major contribution.*

A. There are no set fees between specialists and writers as to what each one's share should be of the payment for an article or book. It just has to be worked out by the individuals based on what percentage of the final sale each person thinks his work contributed. If you think for example that it was your writing that was 75% responsible for selling the article and the expert's contribution 25%, then propose that proportion to the expert. If you think it was a 50-50 deal, suggest that. Some professionals would feel that their co-byline enhanced their position in the field and would not require a split of the fees.

Confessions Collaborator

Q. *I have some confessions which need revision and I also need help in selling. I would like someone not too expensive but reliable and "on the ball."*

A. Some collaborators who have worked in the confession field advertise in WRITER'S DIGEST. You could write them individually and find out how much they charge for their services.

20. What About Author's Agents?

What is an Agent?

Q. *What is an agent, where are they found, what do they charge, what do they offer, should a totally wet-behind-the-ears neophyte have one or should a writer stumble along in the dark? How do I get one, when and if I want one?*

A. An agent, sometimes called a literary agent or an author's agent, is someone who handles the marketing and sales of your work. They are found, usually in New York or California, but occasionally in other states, and they are listed—along with their policies and specialties—in WRITER'S MARKET. Agents usually charge ten percent of sales, and a higher percentage for material sold in the foreign markets. Some offer additional services such as editing, rewriting, or manuscript criticism, for which they charge additional fees. New writers are often advised to market their own work when they are just starting out, since through this process they will become familiar with the markets and needs of these markets. WRITER'S DIGEST advises beginning writers, especially, not to seek an agent "until what you've written is selling so fast and so often that you don't have time to market your own writing." That's when you need the services of an agent. When you're selling and being assigned work faster than you get it in the typewriter and in the mails—an agent is a necessity. There is no need to stumble along in the dark if you study the market well. When you need an agent, select one or two from WRITER'S MARKET, write them and take your time in making the choice. But please don't write WRITER'S DIGEST asking which agent is for you.

Choosing an agent is a personal procedure. It takes a close study of what the agent offers, the type of material you are writing, and it's difficult for another person to recommend an agent. You must make that choice yourself.

Percentages Derived from Sales

Q. *I've noticed that sometimes an author's agent will advertise in* WRITER'S DIGEST, *but won't be listed in* WRITER'S MARKET. *Why are some agents included in one publication, but not in the other?*

A. To qualify for a free listing in WRITER'S MARKET, an agent must derive the greater part of his annual income directly from selling books and articles for clients. Some agents handle other work, such as editing, rewriting, literary criticism, etc. If a literary (author's) agent doesn't derive at least 50% or more of his annual income from direct sale of client's materials, he will not be listed in WRITER'S MARKET. Also, under WRITER'S DIGEST's advertising policy, an agent whose greater income is from literary services rather than sales will be so named, and not called an "agent."

List of Agents

Q. *Where can I get a list of names and addresses of author's agents?*

A. Author's agents are listed in WRITER'S MARKET. The listing tells what kinds of material the agent specializes in, what fees are charged, if any, for reading the new writer's work and what percentage is taken in commission for sales of client materials. A list of names and addresses of literary agents appears in the *Literary Market Place,* available in most libraries. But most of these agents only work with already established writers.

Once and For All

Q. *If a writer authorizes an agent to sell one or more of his works, is the author committed to pay a fee to said agent for writing he subsequently sells himself?*

A. Normally, if an author takes on an agent, he usually is committed to pay the agent a fee for any of his work which is sold after that date, unless there is an agreement between them specifically exempting from commission any work sold by the author himself.

Two Agents?

Q. *Can you tell me whether it is ethical to have two agents? In this case one in Los Angeles, and one in New York. Each handles the same type of material, but in his own locale. Do agents frown on this procedure even though the material submitted to each is not the same?*

A. It is more ethical to have only one agent handling all your material of the same type. Confidence in your agent should not be limited by geographical boundaries. If one specializes in books and the other in TV scripts, that would be another matter.

Agency Problem

Q. *I paid a literary agency for criticism-analysis of two children's stories. They notified me of the opinions of various publishers; but when I asked to whom they showed these stories, they didn't answer my letter. Did I have a right to ask the names of the publishers?*

A. You did indeed. Any reputable agency would not hesitate to reveal the publishers to whom they had submitted material.

One Agent At A Time

Q. *If a book or story is in the hands of an agent, is it possible to make such arrangements that a copy may be submitted to another agent or to a publisher while it is still in the hands of the first agent?*

A. Once a manuscript has been turned over to one agent, it is not ethical to submit copies either to another agent or to a publisher. If you feel the agent is not handling your work to your satisfaction, ask for its return and you shall then be free to try marketing it yourself or to place it with another agent.

Return of Manuscript

Q. *Where an agency ignores a request to return a book manuscript, other than continuing to write letters, what recourse does a writer have? Is there some organization set up for the protection of writers to whom they might appeal?*

A. The best procedure is to write a registered letter to the agency stating that you are withdrawing the manuscript from their consideration and resubmitting it elsewhere. You'll have to retype the manuscript, but it will save you much more in time and frustration. WRITER'S DIGEST would like to be notified whenever you have difficulty getting either payment or reports on your manuscripts, so we can check this information with other complaints in our file and delete the publication from WRITER'S MARKET (if it is listed) or warn readers of the publication's practices in WRITER'S DIGEST.

Handle on Speculation?

Q. *I have many manuscripts and all need to be revised. But I'm on a pension and haven't money to pay for the work. Is there anyone who will revise and sell, take out their share of the money and send me the rest?*

A. No agent is willing or financially able to do revision work on speculation, in the hope that he will be paid eventually out of the sale of the work. Perhaps eventually, by studying WRITER'S DIGEST and the magazines to which you would like to submit, you will be able to learn to revise your own manuscripts and resubmit them for sale. Good luck!

Becoming an Agent

Q. *Can you tell me what the requirements are for becoming a literary agent or tell me where I may obtain such information?*

A. The requirements for becoming a literary agent are those of knowing the publishing market so well that you can prove to prospective clients that you are able to successfully place the work of professional writers with magazine and book editors. Many literary agents came to their jobs after successfully marketing their own work or through being editors in the field and knowing what publishers want to buy.

Agents for Puzzles?

Q. *Are there—and if so, who are they—agencies that handle crosswords, crostics and double crostics?*

A. Most agents are interested only in handling authors who do books, television scripts and other more profitable-length manuscripts. The financial return on items such as crosswords, filler material, poetry, etc. is so small, no agencies can afford to handle just those. There are, of course, a great many magazines which use crossword puzzles other than crossword puzzle magazines themselves. They are listed throughout WRITER'S MARKET.

Recommended List?

Q. *How will I know whether an agent is reputable or not? Is there a printed list I can obtain of recommended agents? I am uncertain as to the qualifications of the company who is representing my interests and I would like to check on its qualifications. The comparative group I have in mind is the Better Business Bureau for companies. Would they also handle literary agents?*

A. Yes, a Better Business Bureau in the city in which your prospective literary agent is located, could let you know whether they have had any complaints about their business operation. The other way you could check on the reputation of the agent is to ask him to give you the names and addresses of three of his clients whom you could write for information about his work with them.

Agents for Illustrators?

Q. *Could you provide me with the names and addresses of agents who represent illustrators, artists, and photographers?*

A. The Manhattan Yellow Pages lists artists' agents and photographers' agencies. No doubt your local public library has a copy of the Manhattan Yellow Pages you could consult. Also see *Artist's Market* and *Photographer's Market* (Writer's Digest Books).

21. Poetry

Poetry Not Selling?

Q. *I have yet to sell one piece of poetry. What are some of the reasons poetry doesn't sell today?*

A. It isn't original enough. Poets want to write about the everyday human emotions that stir us all—the birth of a baby, impending death, the strange quality that we call charisma—but unless the poet brings some really imaginative insight or language to the reader on the subject, the editor won't buy it. In some cases, poetry has faulty construction or uneven meter. You've probably read many books on the principles of poetry, but it doesn't hurt to review them once in a while and read the poetry in the magazines you want to sell to, to analyze what it is about those poems that made the editor buy them. Are there any magazines that print the kinds of poetry you like to read? If so, they're the ones to shoot for!

Poetry Definitions

Q. *What is the difference between free verse and blank verse? Is rhyming in either necessary or optional?*

A. Blank verse is unrhymed five foot iambic verse. Free verse does not follow any of the patterns of alternating accents and unaccents of metric verse. It sets up a music all its own which is neither a measured beat nor haphazard prose. As a general rule, lines that are not metric verse, accent verse or prose ... are probably free verse. Free verse can be rhymed (as in some of Ogden Nash's work), but most frequently it isn't. Blank verse is not rhymed. For additional help with versification, consult *Wood's Unabridged Rhyming Dictionary.*

Manuscript Style

Q. *How should I prepare my manuscript when I'm submitting a poem? Should the byline be just beneath the title or in the upper right-hand corner?*

A. Type your name and address in the upper left-hand corner. The title of your poem should be centered above the body of the poem. Then you should center the poem on the page, with about equal distances above and below, and approximately the same margins to the left and right. You should double-space short poems, but you can use single-spacing on long poems. As a last line, your byline should be typed off to the right so that it ends about where your average line ends.

Resubmit?

Q. *My great-grandfather was a poet and published a book of poems. He had only 300 books printed and gave them out to friends. The copyright was out years ago, over 60 years. There are some wonderful poems in this book and I would like to see them reprinted. Would it be legal to take these poems and have them reprinted in magazines where everyone could enjoy them? If this would be legal, would I still use his name on them or my own?*

A. You could try to bring these poems to the attention of current magazines, but under no condition would it be ethical to sign your name to them. They are the original work of your great-grandfather and should remain so.

Books of Poetry

Q. *I have what I consider a worthwhile manuscript of poetry. Aren't there any publishers that would consider publishing it on a straight royalty basis?*

A. Yes, there are publishers who have a regular royalty contract for poetry books, (see the WRITER'S MARKET list of Book Publishers). However, some of them hesitate to gamble on an unknown poet, and would prefer to publish poets with established reputations. To lay the groundwork for the possible future publication of your book, it would be helpful for you to get your poems published in magazines first.

Newspaper Poetry

Q. *Does it make good sense to publish a poem in a newspaper—for a few dollars or maybe for free—and thereby lose all your copyright protection?*

A. Few newspapers are copyrighted with an overall copyright that covers the entire contents (other than straight hard news, which cannot be copyrighted, of course), so you do lose copyright protection on poetry published in this manner. It wouldn't be to your advantage to put your poetry in the public domain for a few dollars and lose the future use of the poem yourself.

Resell Poems

Q. *A few years ago, I had a volume of poetry published at my own expense. Fortunately, there was a very good sale of this book. Now I would like to submit some poems published in the book to certain magazines, but have hesitated to do so as I'm not sure if this is permissible.*

A. As long as the volume of poetry you had published at your own expense was copyrighted, then all rights to the poems still belong to you. It would be advisable to let the magazine editor know that your submission originally appeared in book form.

Modern Poetry

Q. *I don't understand most modern poetry. Is there some book which has taken these kinds of poems apart, analyzed them and discussed what the poet is saying?*

A. Yes, *The Poet and the Poem*, by Judson Jerome (Writer's Digest Books), has chapters on this subject along with discussions of other matters of interest to poets attempting to become "professional" poets.

Offbeat Poetry

Q. *What can I say? I have a poetry column in a local journal. Some of my recent poetry is unrhymed and has no regular rhythm. Readers constantly hound me with the comments, "That's a poem?" or "It doesn't rhyme!" or "It has no set rhythm!" The truth of the matter is, I have sold more so-called "offbeat" poetry than the "perfect" poem. What can I say to my readers?*

A. Tell them you are writing free verse ... because that *is* what you're doing. Point out to those readers that this is an accepted literary tradition, followed by Walt Whitman and T. S. Eliot, to name just two. No apologies are necessary!

Books of Poetry

Q. *Could you tell me the procedure for an author to sell a book of collected poems, if some of the verse has already been sold to magazines and newspapers? Can he go ahead and have the book published, or must he seek permission of the companies that published his verse?*

A. Yes, the author who intends to collect his poetry, some of which has already been published, into a book, must seek permission from the companies that published the verses originally. There is usually no problem in getting permission, but it's necessary to write for it before producing the book. Poems which were published in an uncopyrighted newspaper would have to be rewritten, since the originals are now in the public domain.

Missing Authors

Q. *I am writing a small book of poems, and I wish to include a few poems given to me by a friend. She told me the lady who wrote the poems never published them. Both my friend and the writer are dead. I tried to contact the writer's sister but the postmaster did not know her. Probably she has passed on. Should I use these poems in my book?*

A. It is not advisable that you use the poems given to you by a friend, since their publication with the author's byline might turn up some heirs who would frown on the use of this work. You seem to have made an effort to locate the author's sister, but you might open yourself to a legal problem here if you include these few poems.

Idea Borrowing

Q. *I have written and sold a poem based on an idea which I do not believe was original. Is such a borrowing considered unethical?*

A. Set your mind at ease. Ideas cannot be copyrighted, so you have done nothing unethical.

22. Song Titles and Lyrics

Songwriting

Q. *I feel that I have a talent for songwriting, and have composed many songs in my spare time, just for the fun of it. Now, I would like to get serious about it. How can I inexpensively protect my material until I find out if it's any good?*

A. Protect your songs by registering them for copyright. The price is ten dollars per song and you can write for application blanks to the Register of Copyrights, Library of Congress, Washington, D.C. 20559.

Music Markets?

Q. *Where can I get a list of music markets? I write a great deal of music, and you used to list such markets.*

A. We had to discontinue carrying the list of music publishers in WRITER'S MARKET because the song business, as you know, has changed so radically in the last few years. Most songs today have to be sold in person to record company representatives rather than to music publishers. It's very hard to deal with this market by mail. The addresses of record companies appear in *The International Buyer's Guide,* published by *Billboard Magazine,* 9000 Sunset Blvd., Los Angeles 90069. For more information, SASE to WRITER'S DIGEST for the reprint, "Breaking into Songwriting," by Jim Fragale.

Copyrighting Songs

Q. *Does the Library of Congress Circular No. R22 cover only books, or songs also?*

A. Circular No. R22 deals mainly with Searches for Copyright and covers musical works as well as books. There is also Circular No. 67 that concerns the copyright registration of poems and song lyrics.

Song Title Protection

Q. *I have several proposed titles to songs that ought to be popular, and suggested lyrics for them, but I fear if they are sent to song-writing people, I'll have no protection. If I get a song copyrighted, the title can still be snatched, can't it?*

A. Titles as such are not subject to copyright. However, it is possible to get the lyrics copyrighted. There is a free circular, No. 67, entitled "Poems and Song Lyrics," which you may obtain by writing to the Copyright Office, Library of Congress, Washington, D.C., 20559. This will tell you what can be copyrighted in this field and which forms to request.

How to Sell Songs

Q. *How does one go about getting his lyrics set to music and subsequently published as a song?*

A. There are companies which, for a fee, will write the music for your lyrics and/or make a "demo" record for you. Some of them advertise in writers' magazines, and publications such as *Songwriter's Review,* 1697 Broadway, New York 10019. The publishing of songs has changed so completely in recent years that it is almost impossible to do it by mail. The writer has to be on the scene in New York, Los Angeles, or Nashville and contact the artists and repertoire representatives of the individual record companies with demo records, since they are the ones to whom most songs are sold originally these days, rather than to publishers.

23. Mailing Rules

Special Fourth Class Rate

Q. *I have been mailing book manuscripts at the special fourth class rate, and understand that article manuscripts qualify, but may short story manuscripts be mailed at this rate? Novelettes? Full-length novels? Book queries with outline and sample chapters?*

A. The special fourth class rate may be used for any fiction or non-fiction manuscripts regardless of length, and also for sample chapters and outlines. If you enclose a letter, be sure you add first class postage to the special rate, and mark the envelope "First Class Letter Enclosed." And remember that unless special fourth class mail is marked "Return Postage Guaranteed," the Post Office may destroy your manuscript if it happens to be mailed to an addressee who cannot be located.

New Name?

Q. *I have submitted many articles and pictures over the years but at infrequent intervals I get the impression that some of the postal officials do not understand the accepted regulations concerning the mailing of manuscripts and photos. Just today I had a story and photos returned from an editor and the mailman required an additional 17¢ for it, although I had placed the required postage on the return envelope which was addressed to me. I had affixed a label and had rubber stamped the return envelope "Educational Material."*

I know that this carries another designation of late, but I had forgotten how it should be indicated.

A. The original designation of "Educational Material" has now been changed to "Special Fourth Class Rate—Manuscript."

Certified and Registered

Q. *Can you explain the difference between "certified mail" and "registered mail"? And when is it necessary to use special types of mail when submitting manuscripts to various markets?*

A. Certified mail is used primarily when you just want a record of receipt of mail at a certain address. It's handled just like regular mail, but a signed receipt is mailed back to you. Registered mail is used to send valuables such as stock certificates and jewelry, because the post office signs a receipt when *they* get it and they know where the package is at all times. Certified mail is the least expensive sure way to requery a publisher, follow up on a manuscript that's been held too long by an editor or withdraw a manuscript. A receipt is sent back to you, so you have a record the editor received your correspondence. That record should be kept in your files. Of course, you wouldn't use either of these methods when initially sending manuscripts to editors. For more information, ask for the booklet, *A Consumer's Guide to Postal Services and Products* at your post office, or write for a copy to the Consumer Advocate, U.S. Postal Service, Washington, D.C. 20260.

Tracing Lost Manuscripts

Q. *I sent a manuscript to a magazine listed in* WRITER'S MARKET. *I waited for a reply for three months, then sent them a letter asking about the status of my manuscript. I received a card saying that they had no record of such a manuscript, that it most likely got lost in the mail. Fortunately, I do have a carbon copy of the manuscript. Is there any way of tracing a lost manuscript?*

A. If your manuscript was sent at the special fourth class rate it can't be traced because the post office is not under obligation to return it to the sender, if for some reason it was misaddressed or undeliverable. If your manuscript was sent first class, then yes, you can ask the post office where you mailed it to put a tracer on it. Keep in mind, though, that magazines are not responsible for unsolicited manuscripts.

24. Rejection Slips

Comments on Rejection Slips

Q. *On recent rejection slips from greeting card companies were handwritten messages, "terrific possibilities but more punch" and "ideas good but lack sales appeal." I am in the dark as to what comprises "punch" and "sales appeal." Should I take these handwritten remarks on form rejections to be encouraging or do editors often write remarks?*

A. These handwritten nutshell criticisms certainly should be regarded as encouraging. By referring to "punch" and "sales appeal," these editors probably meant that your work lacked the impact necessary to make the prospective card buyer immediately react favorably to the cards. It would seem, then, that your underlying ideas are good, but you need to present them in a more colorful, more entertaining or dramatic way that will catch the customer's attention and make him buy.

Rejected?

Q. *My first story was recently returned. It did not have the usual printed rejection slip attached. Instead, I received a short personal note telling me the publication was overstocked and I should not submit material until late August. Was my story rejected completely or should I feel it was adequate for their magazine?*

A. It is possible that your story was not even read, but that it was automatically returned because the market is so overstocked at present. You should resubmit the story in late August, as they suggested, since the note seems noncommittal about rejecting or accepting it.

How to Use Them

Q. *How many rejection slips do you consider the cutoff point— where you give up on that particular article?*

A. If the idea for the article was good enough at the onset for you to take time and work to produce the finished manuscript, you should not abandon it too soon. Rather, learn to look at the rejection slips as bits of advice for improving the original manuscript. Glean whatever an editor jots down as the reason for rejecting the article or story—and improve, revise, take from or add to, until the piece is sold. Rejections, if used properly, can be learning lessons to improve your writing. Be sure to send your work to the appropriate market. Sending an article to a market that is completely unsuitable is a mistake that many beginners make, but marketing—just as writing—is a skill that one learns from experience and study. Some ideas and manuscripts have to be set aside after a dozen or so submissions because either the market isn't ready for them—or they're not ready for today's market.

Resubmitting after Rejection

Q. *Is it ever advisable to submit a story more than once to a magazine that has rejected it?*

A. If the editor tells you he's rejecting it because he's overbought at the time, or he's bought something similar recently—it isn't at all impossible to sell that piece to the same market at a later date. If you wait one year before resubmitting, you may have a chance. But that's only if the rejection letter sounded hopeful, and gave good, sound reasons for rejection. Also, editors change jobs and a new editor may buy what a previous editor rejected.

25. Getting Along With Editors

Acknowledge Acceptance?

Q. *When a manuscript is accepted for publication, should you make any response to the editor—such as "Hooray!"? If so, should it be on acceptance, on receiving your check, or on publication?*

A. Though a response isn't mandatory, if your overwhelming joy, gratitude or surprise needs an outlet, by all means write a note when you learn of your manuscript's acceptance. The editor will be glad you're glad.

They Changed My Story

Q. *I wrote a piece for a certain magazine. It took a year before it was published, but when it did come out, well, they spelled my name right, but that was about it. The style was hacked apart until there was no style. What's more, facts were altered, so the reader was bound to get an impression different from what I had intended. Is it possible for an unknown to get the last word on manuscript revisions?*

A. If an editor changed the intent of your piece, he was overstepping editorial bounds. Some editors show galley proofs to authors; others do not. It would be unusual for an unknown writer to get final approval of his article.

How Long?

Q. *How long may a publisher hold a manuscript? I submitted an unsolicited article to a professional magazine and was told one year later to be patient for another few months because the article would probably be published in July. Fee was not discussed. Now it's August and I wonder how long should I be "patient"?*

A. If an editor has accepted an article and it hasn't appeared within 18 months, it is reasonable for the writer to inquire of the editor whether it will be published and, if not, inform him that you would like to submit it elsewhere.

One Editor Replaces Another

Q. *Is one editor liable for another editor's commitment? When an editor assigns something to a writer or offers payment for a manuscript, then leaves the magazine staff, is the replacement editor liable for that assignment or payment?*

A. There are no rules of war on this one. Often it depends on the terms of departure for the editor. If he is fired, chances are his replacement or his old boss wants to disregard his editorial thinking—perhaps that was the reason for his dismissal. If he was promoted, transferred, or if he departed on good terms, there is likely to be more transitional grace, and old projects and commitments may be honored. The writer's best bet here is to summarize the situation in a letter to the previous editor's replacement, including copies of all correspondence. The new editor then will be in a position to judge whether he wants to keep the writer on assignment or kill the idea. Whether this is accompanied by a kill fee (usually 20% of the anticipated payment for the piece) depends on whether a kill fee was part of the original agreement and how far the writer has gone with the idea. If an article has in fact been written on assignment for a previous editor and a kill fee was agreed on, this may have to be discussed with the publication's publisher or owner. Most editors are honorable most of the time, and they will be fair with the writer. But when a magazine staff changes, it is often because the publisher is unhappy with earlier staffers—and it can signal a new editorial direction for the publication.

Story Acceptance

Q. *What happens when a story is accepted by a magazine? Does the writer just get a check in the mail or are there preliminaries to go through, such as signing some paper regarding rights or originality?*

A. The writer is customarily notified of acceptance by mail. The check may be included or may follow later, depending on the policy of the publisher. Check WRITER'S MARKET for information on what rights the magazine buys, or ask the editor. The editor assumes the writer is the story's originator, so there is rarely any paper to sign to this effect.

Editors Explain Rejections?

Q. *After four years of freelance writing and not having sold a word, I would like a personal remark from an editor on why the manuscript didn't qualify, instead of the usual cold-blooded rejection slip. Is there a special approach you can recommend?*

A. Most new writers need objective help in discovering the flaws that prevent their work from selling. But an editor's job is to find publishable material, not to explain rejections. Considering the thousands of manuscripts that yearly cross an editor's desk, personal analysis would be impossible. For constructive criticism, join a writer's club or use a criticism service, such as the Writer's Digest Criticism Service.

SASE with a Query?

Q. *Should one always SASE with a query? After receiving a favorable reply to a query, how soon will the editor expect the manuscript?*

A. It's always a good idea to SASE with the query. When an editor gives you a favorable response on an article idea and doesn't specify a deadline, it's up to you to decide how quickly you can get it finished. Acknowledge his letter with a note saying when you will deliver the article.

Waiting Time

Q. *How long should I wait for an editor's decision on my manuscript? How do I follow up on an article that's being held by an editor an unusually long time?*

A. Depending on a magazine's staff and the amount of mail it gets, an editor may take from three weeks to two months to report on submissions. A book editor may require three months or longer. Check WRITER'S MARKET for specific reporting times. Remember that when an editor says he reports in six weeks, that means six weeks from the time he receives your manuscript. If you live on one coast and he's on the other, it may have taken a week to reach him. If you've had no report from an editor by the maximum reporting time, send a brief inquiry asking if your manuscript or query is still being considered. Include the story title, date of original submission, and brief description of the piece. SASE. In the rare case where a publisher fails to report even after your inquiry, send a certified letter to the editor, advising that you are withdrawing your manuscript from that publication's consideration so you may submit it elsewhere. Be sure to notify WRITER'S MARKET editors of the problem, so they can keep their files up-to-date on the bad habits of some publishers.

Editor-Author Relations

Q. *As the editor of a literary magazine, do I have the right to make changes in accepted manuscripts, with or without the author's approval?*

A. Ethically, an editor should discuss any *significant* changes with the author.

What Do They Mean?

Q. *I keep getting personal letters from editors saying my manuscripts are interesting, but "not quite right for us." What does this statement mean? If it's so interesting, why isn't it right?*

A. These letters expressing interest are meant to encourage you and show you your work does have a degree of promise. The material's style or content, however, may not be in keeping with the magazine's editorial requirements, or something similar may have recently been published. Get to know the markets better by studying what these publishers are buying.

Resell Same Article?

Q. *If I sell an article with pictures to a magazine, can I sell the same article again to another magazine?*

A. If the first magazine bought first rights only, then yes, you can resell. If you attempt to resell the piece after the first magazine buys and *before* they print it—you will, of course, have to be sure you're completely reslanting the piece so the editor who bought first rights will have no cause for complaint if the articles are published simultaneously. It's always safest to advise the second editor that another aspect of this subject was treated by you in an article bought by another magazine, since he may feel the two publications are in competition.

Visit the Editor?

Q. *As an unpublished writer, I would like to know if one must usually go see the fiction editor personally.*

A. A writer should not visit the fiction editor at all. It is best to send the manuscript by mail, with SASE for its safe return in case it's not published.

Did He Mean It?

Q. *Recently, a manuscript was returned by an editor who had previously taken ten of my stories. He wrote, "Although we like your story quite a bit, we unhappily have no space left for the current publishing year's issues. We will, however, be considering manuscripts again along about New Year's for next year." Would I be justified in holding my manuscript until January and submitting it again?*

A. Take him at his word and resubmit your story, perhaps with a tactful note reminding him of how much he liked it. If he had meant to flatly reject it, it isn't likely he would have added that sentence about considering manuscripts the first of the year.

Rubber Stamp?

Q. *Every time a writer submits a story he, in effect, is obliged to extend to the publisher what amounts to an option ad infinitum on the manuscript. I am thinking of getting the following rubber stamp made: "This manuscript is offered to you for sale, with an option of purchase terminating in 30 days from date." What would the publisher have to say about that?*

A. That depends on the publisher. There are book publishers, for example, who normally take about 90 days to report on a manuscript, so in such a case, your rubber-stamped 30-day ultimatum might bring your manuscript back unread. In most cases, particularly with magazine submissions, there should be no objection to such a stamped statement provided it allows a reasonable length of time for consideration of the manuscript. Summon up your patience and try offering 60 days instead of 30.

No Name, No Pay!

Q. *When a magazine advertises payment of a set sum per word, shouldn't they be expected to pay it? True, it was only a six-line* *verse filler, but they did use it! I received no letter of acceptance or rejection. To add insult to injury, they didn't even use my name. How can I be sure this won't happen again to some longer, more important piece?*

A. Perhaps you forgot to put your name and address on your manuscript, as you did on this letter to us! But in any event, you should write to that editor, asking why you received neither byline nor the advertised payment. To be sure this won't happen again, don't submit any future material to this publication. Before you submit to other magazines, you might ask them about their rate of payment for fillers.

Paid But Unpublished

Q. *Is it "cricket" to ask when one might expect something to see print? I've had a number of manuscripts accepted (and paid for) but to my knowledge they have not been published.*

A. A tactful query on your part certainly seems in order. But bear in mind that sometimes, for one reason or another, a paid-for piece never does get into print.

Forgotten Author?

Q. *I'm mystified! Once in awhile I sell a story which the magazine pays for, yet I never see it in print—even though the editor says he will send copies of the issue containing it. I hope you can give me some advice explaining this situation, as I'm typically egotistical enough to want to see my "brainchildren" in published form.*

A. Sometimes magazine editors forget to send copies of stories they published to the original authors. Why not drop a note to each of the editors involved asking for a copy of your story, if it has been published. In some cases, editors change or editor's policies change and although stories are bought, they are not used.

Lost Manuscript

Q. *Is a magazine publisher responsible for stories he received but apparently lost in his office? One of my stories was lost by one of the major magazine publishers. I have a letter from them stating they cannot find it, and I am wondering if I should ask them to pay for it, since I cannot send it elsewhere.*

A. Many magazines go on record as indicating they are not responsible for unsolicited manuscripts, so legally they cannot be charged. Retype another original from your carbon, which you should *always* make!

Plagiarism?

Q. *In December, I submitted an article to a new magazine. The following February, I received a rejection slip with the note: "We are quite taken with your style and would appreciate receiving material from you in the future." I was thrilled even with the rejection in this manner. Then, the August issue of this magazine appeared on the newsstand, bearing an article by the same title. Though the printed article is admittedly better than my submission, being longer and more thoroughly researched, it is similar beyond belief. The title, style, opening and closing paragraphs, and content are almost identical. It is hard for me to accept this as coincidence. Do I have any right to question this similarity?*

A. Many writers get the same idea at the same time and often use the same language in writing. If you think there was some appropriation of your material, though, write the editor and ask for an explanation.

Legal Recourse?

Q. *After reading the outline of my proposed historical novel, a leading publisher asked me to mail a prologue and four chapters. The manuscript was mailed, first class postage enclosed for return. The*

publisher acknowledged receipt, but I did not hear from the publish-
er again. After three months I wrote a letter inquiring as to their
decision. The editorial department replied that my manuscript had
been misfiled; they did not know it had arrived until receipt of my
letter. Within a few weeks the senior editor wrote a vague letter say-
ing the chapters had not lived up to the outline; that the manuscript
was being returned fourth class. *More than two and one-half months*
have passed and the manuscript has not arrived. The publisher says
they have asked the post office to trace it. If the post office is unable
to locate it, as now seems possible, do I have recourse against the
publisher? There's something illogical about the publisher's
explanation.

A. You do not have much recourse. Although this is an unfortunate
experience, you are probably unduly suspicious of the publisher. As
a professional author you undoubtedly kept a carbon of the manuscript, so you might as well forget this experience and start retyping
the manuscript for submission to other publishers.

Withdraw Material?

Q. *Three months ago, I sent some of my best poems to a certain*
publisher, who never acknowledged receiving them. Anxious to put
them back in circulation, I requested their return. My letter was not
acknowledged, nor have the poems been returned. SASE was en-
closed with correspondence. My query is this: may I legitimately
write the editor stating that I withdraw my offer of the poems and
then send them to other editors? Since some of my other verses, (no
better than those in question) have been accepted, I should like to
offer the latter for publication.

A. The procedure is to send the publisher a certified letter indicating
that you are withdrawing from their consideration the poems mailed
on such and such a date. Be sure to list the titles of the poems. You
are then free to resubmit this material elsewhere.

What Mailing Method?

Q. *So many times in the last few years when I mailed stories or articles with photos by the special fourth class rate—manuscript, with postage for that rate, my manuscripts were returned to me by first class, with the added postage applied and my own directions crossed out. Does editorial policy frown on the cheaper rate and am I obligated to reimburse the editor? If a writer is regularly sending out many manuscripts, the fourth class rate certainly saves postage. Editorially speaking, do I downgrade my material by using the fourth class rate?*

A. The fact that some of your manuscripts are returned by magazines first class instead of special fourth class rate is to your advantage. It is probably the magazine's policy and you certainly aren't under any obligation to reimburse the editor. The special fourth class rate is an advantage for the writer who is making a great many submissions, especially of packages containing photos, etc., and you do not downgrade your material by sending it at that rate. Editors are understanding about the financial problems of freelance writers and realize it is only being professional to mail material the least expensive way.

Magazine and Book Marketing

Q. *While my nonfiction book is circulating among publishers, may I try to sell parts of it as magazine articles? If so, how do I mark the article manuscript? The book manuscript? If I mark an article "First Rights," what happens if the book is published before the article is printed? Some of my articles have stayed in editors' files for years before coming to light.*

A. Yes, you should mark your article manuscripts First Serial Rights Only while your nonfiction book is circulating among publishers. If you do subsequently sell the book, and it is published before an article you have also sold sees the light of day, then you should write the magazine editor and explain the circumstances. Since they would, in effect, only be buying second serial rights, at that point, they may wish to ask that a portion of their payment be returned.

Nudge Editor?

Q. *To the unestablished writer, marketing becomes as difficult, or more so, than the creative effort. My particular problem is trying to place timely or seasonal material. The classic example was a Christmas poem I mailed in August to a top publication, which returned the poem the following February. There was no acknowledgment of a letter I had written to say I was sending the poem elsewhere. Would sending topical material by registered mail help, or would this antagonize an editor?*

A. When sending topical material, just include in a covering letter a brief request that since the material is timely, the author would appreciate a reply by a specific date. This won't help in every case, but it may reduce your frustrations with a few editors.

Free Critique?

Q. *Can editors be counted on to give authors any hints as to why their stories fail to sell?*

A. Whether editors will give advice to authors on why they are rejecting stories depends on the time they have available to offer this kind of personal criticism to writers they feel hold future promise. Unfortunately, most editors are so harrassed by too much work and so little time that they are not able to provide this service.

How Long To Wait?

Q. *What is the reasonable amount of time one should wait for a purchased article to be published? I sold an article to a monthly publication a year ago, was paid for it, but it has not yet appeared in print. The material could be slightly dated by now. If a magazine* purchased a piece and then decided not to use it, would they return it to me? Would I then be obligated to return the money (long since spent, of course)?

A. If a magazine has not published material it has bought within 12 months, the writer should ask the magazine to return it for republishing elsewhere and be permitted to retain the original fee paid for it. This guideline is used by the American Society of Journalists & Authors, Inc. and you might mention this to the publisher of the magazine that bought your material.

Multiple Query

Q. *My partner and I have collaborated on a children's book. She is doing the text and I am doing the illustrating. We sent several query letters to different publishers to see if they were interested in the material. We received a letter from a publisher who said he would like to see the material immediately, so we sent it to him. In the meantime, we have received answers to all our letters, all saying they are interested and would like to see the material. Can you tell us the best way to answer these letters? Also, can you tell us approximately what the going rate is on a book of this type? Approximately what can the writer expect to receive and what does the illustrator receive?*

A. You should write each publisher saying your manuscript is currently in the hands of another publisher and, as soon as it is returned, you will send it on to them. As for royalties, they range from ten to 15% with splits between author and illustrator varying depending on amount of work by each.

26. Writing Plays

Comparative Dialog

Q. *I am writing a play on a historical character. How would I incorporate exact quotations of his and other characters into my own dialog? For example, in a papal brief I think I would have to use the exact words of the Pope and also the exact words of the reply, of personal letters, etc., that are in the public record. How would I do this and also use dialog of my own creation?*

A. Steep yourself in the life and speech of that historical period to the point where there would not be any noticeable difference between the verbatim quotes and the dialog you invent, as Arthur Miller has done in *The Crucible*. Or, impose your own style of speech on the period, paraphrasing the sources to make them sound compatible with your characters' dialog as in George Bernard Shaw's *Saint Joan*.

Books on Playwriting

Q. *I'd like to write a play. Will you recommend a couple helpful books for writers just starting in the field? I'm interested in basic books on how to write the play.*

A. Books you might find useful are *The Art of Dramatic Writing*, by Lajos Egri (Touchstone-Clarion), $2.95 paper and *Playwriting: The Structure of Action*, by Sam Smiley (Prentice-Hall), $7.50 paper. The cover story in the May 1977 issue of WRITER'S DIGEST, "How to Write and Sell That Play," by Tim Kelly, is an excellent how-to article on playwriting.

Playing Time

Q. *What is the actual performing time per page of dialog?*

A. The average playing time of a 20 to 30 minute one-act play is 20 to 30 typewritten double-spaced pages. A 90 minute to two-hour full-length play usually runs 90 to 120 double-spaced typewritten pages.

Play Agent?

Q. *I have been writing one and two-act plays for little theaters. Is there a writer's guild? Is it necessary to send play manuscripts through an agent?*

A. Yes, there is a Writer's Guild of America but it is for radio, TV and film writers. There is the Dramatists Guild of the Authors League of America (234 W. 44th St., New York City 10036). There are many producers who do not require submissions through an agent. For a list of these as well as producers who work only through agents, see the Play Producers section of WRITER'S MARKET.

27. Writing for TV

Writing the TV Script

Q. *What is the proper form for TV scripts for live and filmed productions?*

A. In scripts for live productions, dialog is double-spaced and scene directions typed all caps, single-spaced. Scripts for filmed shows use camera directions in all caps, scene descriptions in caps and lower-case centered on the page. Scene numbers do not appear on the manuscript; these are added to the final draft by the studio. Remember—the right half of the manuscript page is left blank for director's notes.

TV Scripts

Q. *On completion of an hour-long TV script adapted for a program that is filmed in California, would it be wiser to contact an agent in New York or California, or would it make any difference?*

A. If the film producer is located in California, it would be better to work with an agent who is in the same area.

How to Submit

Q. *How does a writer go about submitting his book or short story to a production studio for possible televising as a series?*

A. Most TV producers work through agents who know the markets for various story themes. Check the author's agents section of WRITER'S MARKET for details about agents who work in the TV industry. Also see the July, 1976 issue of WRITER'S DIGEST for Harlan Ellison's informative article, "Writing for Television Today."

TV Script Length?

Q. *Could you please tell me how many typewritten pages are in the average half-hour TV script and the hour-long teleplay?*

A. There are about 30 pages in the half-hour script and double that in the hour-long script.

TV "Treatment" and "Outline"

Q. *What is the difference between "treatment" and "outline"?*

A. An outline is a short, concise synopsis of the story. The "treatment" is a scene-by-scene explanation, indicating the specific action, motivation, possible special effects, etc. It provides a fuller interpretation of the script's potential.

Script Protection

Q. *How can a writer protect a TV script he has submitted to an agent?*

A. Nonmembers of the Writers' Guild of America can mail their scripts to that Guild with a check for seven dollars and have the script's completion date registered. The address of the Writers' Guild, West is 8955 Beverly Boulevard, Los Angeles 90048.

Permission to Adapt

Q. *Several years ago I read a story which I felt had the makings of a TV play. Is this sort of thing done, and if so, whose permission do I have to get? The author's? The magazine's? Do I write the play first and submit it to them, or ask permission to attempt to adapt the story first?*

A. Yes, you'd have to get permission from the original author to do a TV adaptation of the story. Write the author, in care of the magazine in which you saw the story before writing the adaptation, since there is the possibility permission may not be granted.

28. Writing for Motion Pictures

Movie Musical

Q. *When writing a screenplay musical, is it necessary to collaborate with a composer or songwriter or should the writer simply make insertions in the play where a song should enter, describing what flavor the song should have?*

A. Since motion picture producers have their own ideas about who should write the songs for musicals, your best bet would be to simply make insertions in the play where the song should enter, describing the type of song you have in mind. Remember—most motion picture producers will only look at scripts submitted through literary agents.

Movie Scripts

Q. *I am writing a play for the movie industry and need to learn more about the camera shots. I want someone familiar with movie writing to take parts of my play and set them to the proper shots.*

A. Why don't you simply write your story in standard script form and submit it to an accredited agent? Movie companies don't expect the material they buy to be worked out down to the smallest detail. Once your script is sold, the shots would become largely the concern of the director who will have a more practiced and knowing eye in this matter.

Autobiography—Film

Q. *I am writing a story about myself and my early life. I believe my story told in the right way would make an interesting movie. How can I get it into the hands of the right producer? I am writing it in play form. Is this acceptable and where would I send it upon completion?*

A. The play form is acceptable, but motion picture producers and studios will look at original scripts only if they are submitted through recognized agents.

29. Syndicating a Column

Syndicates

Q. *What is a syndicate? How does it serve a writer of factual articles?*

A. A syndicate is a business service that makes a wide variety of features available to many publications. A newspaper syndicate, for example, might sell the same column to 100 different newspapers all over the country. Each newspaper would pay for this column according to the size of its circulation. A nonfiction writer might be able to sell a daily or weekly column do a national syndicate. For a description of the editorial needs and the names and addresses of syndicates, see WRITER'S MARKET. You may also order the *Editor & Publisher Syndicate Directory,* published by Editor & Publisher, 575 Lexington Ave., New York City 10022. Current price is five dollars.

Factual Columns

Q. *I want to syndicate a factual column for a newspaper. How much material would I need to present to the editor of that newspaper? The idea only? A sample? A month or year's worth?*

A. It depends on whether you're suggesting a daily or weekly column. If a daily, then it would be best to have a month's columns ready to show; for a weekly column, have two months' supply written. In both cases have ideas written down for another three to six months' columns.

Self-Syndication?

Q. *Is it wiser to syndicate your own newspaper column or to sell your column to a national syndicate on a royalty basis? What are the advantages of each?*

A. When a writer syndicates his own newspaper column he receives the full amount—not a percentage—of the gross receipts of the sale to newspapers. On the other hand, he must bear the cost of promoting and selling his column. When a writer sells his column to a syndicate he receives a percentage, averaging 40 to 60% of the gross receipts, because the syndicate has done the promoting and selling of the column.

Syndicate Payment

Q. *When a syndicate is said to pay $25, what does this cover?*

A. Such a flat rate usually refers to the payment for a single feature ... a one-shot item rather than a continuing column.

Waiting Time

Q. *When I submit a feature to a syndicate, how soon can I expect a decision? How can I make sure I get my percentage of sales?*

A. Most of the syndicates listed in WRITER'S MARKET report on submissions in two weeks to two months. Unless the sum is large enough to warrant sending an auditor to check the accounts, most writers accept the syndicate's statements in good faith, since publishers and syndicates couldn't stay in business long if they weren't honest with their writers.

Simultaneous?

Q. *Somewhere I read that it is permissible to send samples of a column to several syndicates at the same time. Is this correct?*

A. No, the sample columns should be sent to only one syndicate at a time. Perhaps you are thinking of syndicating your own column and in that case, you would send your sample columns simultaneously to the various individual newspaper editors (in non-competing circulation areas, of course).

National vs Local

Q. *I am interested in syndicating my own newspaper column. Will it be necessary for me to copyright the column in my name in order to send it to several different markets? If I must copyright the column in my name, how do I go about doing this?*

A. Yes, it will be necessary for you to copyright the columns in your own name to protect your rights. A practice that has been followed by many national syndicates and persons syndicating their own columns has been to print a book-length collection of columns copyrighted in the author's name. The author then puts the copyright symbol, date and name in the column "reprints" sent to newspapers. This is less expensive than taking out an individual copyright on each column, since there is a ten dollar fee per column, or book. Applications for either can be obtained by writing to the Register of Copyrights, Library of Congress, Washington, D.C. 20559.

Newspaper Column Syndication

Q. *How do you market material for a daily or weekly newspaper column to a syndicate? When readers' comments, which are welcomed, are integrated into the column, do you need the reader's permission before printing his comment or name? How do you protect your idea and your rights? How do you determine a rate and how do you state it when submitting samples? Are there syndicates that purchase fillers? If so, how do you submit them?*

A. Write a query to the editor of the syndicate that best suits your needs, enclose six sample columns and be sure to SASE. Ideas cannot be copyrighted, but once the material is published, it can be registered for copyright protection. If the column clearly invites readers to submit their comments for publication, then there is no need to request permission to quote. The rate of payment is usually fixed by the syndicate, not by the writer. It may be anywhere from 40 to 60% of the gross proceeds; however, there are some syndicates that pay the writer a salary or a minimum guarantee. Yes, there are syndicates that buy fillers. The fillers should be typed individually on separate sheets of paper. If you are not familiar with the various types of syndicates, consult WRITER'S MARKET, which provides a detailed account of each syndicate's payment rate and field of specialization.

Series Humor?

Q. *Is there an outlet for a series of "humorous commentaries" on the condition of modern life? Would it be best to write to a magazine? Is it better to submit articles individually?*

A. Try querying syndicates listed in WRITER'S MARKET that best suit your needs. It might be less difficult however, to place these humorous essays individually in magazines.

Book Rights

Q. *I'd like to write a number of articles in the form of letters about a street I've lived on for 17 years. If these letters were acceptable to a syndicate, suppose I later want them put in a book? How would I present them to a syndicate with such a thought in mind—regarding later use?*

A. Simply specify that you wish to retain book rights.

30. Finding Addresses

Book Authors

Q. *How can I find the address of an author? I would like to tell an author how much I enjoyed his book.*

A. You can write to the author in care of his publisher. Book publishers will not usually divulge addresses of their authors, but they will forward mail addressed to them.

Short Story and Article Writers

Q. *How can I get in touch with someone who has written an article in a magazine I've read?*

A. Write to the author in care of the magazine in which the article or short story appeared. Most editors will forward any mail received which is addressed to contributing writers. Magazines, though, usually have a policy of not giving out the addresses of their contributors.

31. Publishing Procedures

Mysteries—How Long?

Q. *A close friend insists an editor will not accept a mystery novel (not a who-done-it) if it exceeds 50,000 words. My novel will exceed this amount by 10-20,000 words. Will an editor insist I cut my words to reach this requirement?*

A. Editorial requirements are usually more flexible than your friend believes. Some publishers of mysteries will take 70,000 words or more; for specific information, see listings of book publishers in WRITER'S MARKET.

Always Keep a Carbon!

Q. *When a magazine says "assumes no responsibility for unsolicited material," does that mean the editors may not return a manuscript even if SASE is provided?*

A. The magazine will certainly try to send the manuscript back in its return envelope, but if the manuscript or envelope gets misplaced, the magazine cannot be held responsible.

Reprint Buyers

Q. *In the case of such magazines as* Reader's Digest, *do the editors select the articles from perusal of various magazines or do authors submit printed articles they feel might be suitable for reprint?*

A. Though the editors usually select the articles for reprinting, an author may submit tearsheets to bring his material to their attention.

Vocabulary Lists

Q. *I am interested in writing children's stories for the younger set. Where can I obtain a suitable word list for these stories?*

A. Many publishers of trade books for children do not use formal vocabulary lists, but publishers of textbook readers for the primary grades often have very formal restrictions on vocabulary (based on studies made in elementary schools). Consult the publishers themselves for their individual vocabulary requirements. Also, check your local library for books on readability that contain word lists.

Single Copies

Q. *I would like to obtain sample copies of a number of magazines not sold locally. To whom do I address such a request, and is payment expected?*

A. Send your request to the editor, and offer to pay for the sample copy if necessary. Some magazines charge; others don't. Be sure to SASE in case they do need further correspondence with you.

Chain Publishers

Q. *There are cases where a publisher will issue several magazines, all of the same type, editorial style and content, from the same address. (They have different titles, though.) In such cases, when a writer is submitting material for use in these magazines, is the material considered for all magazines published by that company, even though it is addressed to one particular magazine? Or is it in order to resubmit it for consideration to another magazine, even though it is published by the same company? I ask this because I do not want to make the mistake of submitting material to more than one magazine published*

by the same company, if it is not proper to do so after having re-
ceived a rejection from one of them.

A. You are right. Certain editors head more than one magazine for
their publisher, but from the same address. Also, an editor will pass
along to another editor at the same company any story he can't use
but thinks the other editor might want.

Juveniles Seasonal?

Q. *Is there a special time of year that material is read and accepted*
by publishers of children's books? If not, how far ahead should sea-
sonal material be sent?

A. Most publishers read manuscripts year-round. Seasonal material
should be submitted at least one year ahead of time.

Back to the Author?

Q. *After a publisher accepts a manuscript, does he proofread it and*
send it back to the writer for corrections and retyping?

A. If you are talking about simple grammatical corrections, the publisher takes care of this and does not return the manuscript to the
author for retyping. Where substantial revisions of ideas or style are
suggested, the manuscript may be returned to the author for additional work.

Special Meaning?

Q. *A children's story of mine was recently rejected. Instead of the*
usual rejection slip in the return envelope with the manuscript, I re-
ceived a letter saying my manuscript was sent under separate cover.
When I received it, it was insured. I did not send it insured. Does
this have any special meaning that my manuscript has any merit that
would interest another publisher?

A. Some publishers just have the company policy of returning manuscripts insured. If the original company had any special comments to make on its merits, they would have said so in their rejection letter. Do not hesitate, however, to send it to another publisher right away.

Offer to Buy

Q. *After submitting a 2,000-word article to a magazine, I received a letter of acceptance saying they were buying 500 words of the article at five cents a word, a check for $25 enclosed. At first I thought of rejecting this offer, but as the article had been on the rounds for some time I decided against it. I am still not sure how I stand on this matter, though. Is this a usual procedure, or should a publisher pay for the whole article even if he only wants 500 words? And what about the remaining 1500 words? Are they still my property to be offered for sale again by me?*

A. A publisher who is not able to use a full article may offer to buy a part of it from the writer. If the writer accepts, then he agrees to the terms. The balance of the article can be sold to a *noncompetitive* market by the writer.

Reporting Time

Q. *How long does a book publisher take to report on a manuscript?*

A. The best you can expect is one month from the time you mail the material. Seven weeks is average. Two months is not unusual. Check WRITER'S MARKET for reporting times of various publishers. After that length of time, send a brief query, enclosing SASE. If you still do not hear from the publisher, you may want to withdraw the book from his consideration.

32. Foreign Language Translations

Resell Foreign Story

Q. *I speak and read French and found a marvelous short story in a foreign magazine I'd like to translate and sell to an American magazine. How do I do it?*

A. If you have a facility with another language and would like to submit a translation of a foreign short story, you must write the publication in which the foreign story appeared and get permission of both the author and the publisher to do your translation. Whether you would be required to share payment from the American publisher depends on what arrangements you make with them. It's always wisest to clarify this point before you approach any American editor so there is no delay if he is interested in your idea.

Translation Markets

Q. *What are the markets for translations of foreign stories, articles and books?*

A. Few magazines directly indicate their interest in translation material, but there's no reason not to try any magazine whose subject matter is similar to what you propose. (See procedure to follow in answer above.) A few book publishers have published translations of previously-published foreign works. To find out who these book publishers are, see the *Subject Guide to Books in Print* under the categories of French language and literature. Note names of publishers. Other languages are similarly listed.

Translator Job

Q. *How does one get a job as a translator? I speak German and English equally well and am also an aspiring writer. Could I start by translating technical articles or books? If so, how?*

A. Translation jobs are available primarily with companies that have technical reports and correspondence to translate, although a few book publishers might be prospects. A professional association of translators could supply additional information. Contact the American Translators Association, P.O. Box 129, Croton-on-Hudson, New York City, 10520. Another contact is a clearing house for translators and publishers, The Translation Center, Columbia University, 307A Math B, 116 St. & Broadway, New York City 10027.

List of Translators?

Q. *Is there any published listing of translators with details on which languages they're proficient in? I'd like to see if my qualifications would be acceptable to obtain such a listing.*

A. Yes, there is a listing of translators in the directory, *Literary Market Place.* You could send your qualifications to the editor of that directory, published by R.R. Bowker Co., 1180 Avenue of the Americas, New York City 10036.

33. Avoiding Plagiarism

Quote How Much?

Q. *In several articles I have written I quoted briefly from hardcover editions of writings of several doctors. In most cases I referred to the doctor by name, his book, and the publisher. Would you please tell me how much I can quote without writing for special permission?*

A. There are no hard and fast rules on fair use. Some publishers say that, for example, if a whole poem is quoted, as few as 25 words may be a copyright infringement, while other publishers—especially in the scholarly field—say 500 words is allowable, as long as you give proper credit to the author and publisher. One of the guides writers use in deciding how much they can quote is to apply this question to their material: Is what I am using impairing the sale value of the original?

Free To Use?

Q. *Some time ago my husband and I bought in an antique shop, a notebook of original poetry by Francis McAdams, who died in 1942. Are we required to locate his descendants before publishing any of the poetry? His most prolific year of poetry was 1931 and much of it has historical value. Could you give information on how to go about finding descendants if we need to?*

A. Is the book you purchased copyrighted? If so, the copyright line would appear on the fly leaf. If it does appear, the copyright is in force for 28 years from the date of copyright. It also could have been renewed for copyright for another 28 years (and extended if expired since 1962—before the present copyright bill was passed). You are not at liberty to use any material from a book that has been copyrighted if the copyright is still in effect. If you are not sure and want to clarify whether the copyright is still in effect, write the Library of Congress, Washington, D.C. 20559.

Similarity Breeds Suits

Q. *I have been writing a vocabulary column which I would like to sell to small newspapers. Without realizing it, my column is much like the monthly word power column printed in* Reader's Digest, *by Peter Funk. In fact, although I am not using the words in his two books,* Thirty Days to a More Powerful Vocabulary *and* Six Weeks to Words of Power, *my daily vocabulary tests in my written columns* resemble *the vocabulary tests used in his books. Is there a copyright on Funk's column? If I sold my newspaper column, would I have to get permission from Peter Funk? I stress this point: I am not using his words, but my test methods* resemble *his test methods.*

A. If Funk's column is copyrighted separately from *Reader's Digest's* overall copyright, it probably carries the copyright notice somewhere near the title. How closely your vocabulary tests resemble his, of course, would be the crux of the matter. It would be best to consult an attorney for advice on this point.

Rewriting Songs

Q. *I have written a song, taken from, and based on an original poem. Some words are different, while others are words of the original author. I would like to know if this is legal, and if not, how I can get permission from the original author? Could I use the music from another original song or do I need the consent of the composer? I have written "answers" to several hit songs. The words are different, but they fit the original music.*

A. Neither the music from one song nor a number of words from another can be used by you if the copyright is still in effect on either song. Check the directory, *Variety Music Cavalcade* to determine if the copyright is still in effect on the songs in question. This book lists songs by title and tells when the copyright was originally issued. It also gives the name of the publishing company to whom you should write to inquire about permission to use parts of the song.

Newspaper Features

Q. *I have in mind an article about Christmas in a penitentiary for the December issue of a magazine. I am an avid reader of the nearby* Penitentiary News *and have been for over five years. No, I am not a convict or an ex-convict. I've never been inside the pen, and the warden denied my request for a visit to get material. My idea is to quote the prison* News, *which is full of convicts' laments and their sad feelings of being behind prison bars on Christmas Day. I wrote the associate warden for permission to quote the* News, *and he said that I would have to get permission to quote each featured item. His exact words: "Newspaper copy is in the area of public domain so that pick-ups of news from it may be made. Republication of featured items of the* News *however, would have to follow the usual routine of obtaining specific releases for each such item." If I had to go to all that trouble (specific releases for each item) the venture would not be worth it. If I ignored this warning, would I stand to be sued or something?*

A. I'm afraid you have no choice but to write for specific releases for the feature articles by the inmates of the penitentiary, or risk the possibility of suit. For further information on the copyright laws you might want to write the Copyright Office, Library of Congress, Washington, D.C. 20559 and ask for a free copy of their information circular.

Where Research Ends

Q. *For years I've been more or less avoiding nonfiction articles because I don't know where "research" ends and plagiarism begins. Where do you draw the line?*

A. If long passages are lifted verbatim, the writer has to get permission from the copyright owner. But don't let research scare you off. Ideas can't be copyrighted, so after you've researched the facts, simply relate them in your own words.

Is it Plagiarism?

Q. *I read a story in which the main character had many suppositions as to how his adventure would end. None was right. I would like to write a short story using one of these suppositions for my ending. However, of necessity, my story would have to be very close to the original. Is this plagiarism? Can I do it?*

A. It is highly unlikely that the author would allow you to use *his* character in *his* story with a solution that *he* suggested. You'll find that originality is the best way of avoiding plagiarism.

34. Writing and Selling Specialized Material

Epigrams and Proverbs

Q. *I have written several hundred original epigrams and poetical proverbs which I believe are good. Would it be more profitable for me to submit them in manuscript form for book publication, or in small lots to magazines?*

A. Since it is usually easier for a beginner to sell to a magazine rather than a book publisher, it might be to your advantage to send these fillers to magazine markets. If possible, try to retain book rights so that eventually you can publish them as a collection in book form.

True—But Not a Story

Q. *After moving to this city, where the crime rate is unusually high, I've had several frightening narrow escapes. I would like to write about these but they would be short, with no exciting endings. In only one did I exchange words with my would-be attacker. Do you think a magazine would be interested or do you advise that I just forget it?*

A. These first-person experiences could be written as nonfiction articles, but only if they offer sound, constructive new insight into this problem and its solution. This would involve factual research with police departments, safety bureaus and other experts.

Comedy Skits

Q. *Big Name Entertainers have Big Name Writers, but I think my material would be welcome to some little-known comedian. Where can I find names and addresses of such entertainers needing comedy routines, when I live in an area where comedians seldom appear because the natives' chief amusement is listening to the cornstalks popping as they grow or watching pigs fight for a faucet at their mama's dinnerplace?*

A. Provided that your Iowa corn remains in your fields and not in your jokes, several avenues are open to you. Since it's helpful to know a comedian's style of delivery, watch for rising young entertainers on TV shows emceed by Merv Griffin, Mike Douglas and Johnny Carson. You may contact these newcomers in care of those programs. You might also treat yourself to a subscription to *Variety,* the show business newspaper that is sure to mention the names and places where lesser-known comedians appear. In fact, you might get this information from big city newspapers. Write the performers in care of the clubs where they appear.

Historical Sports?

Q. *I write sports articles, mainly covering great football games of 40 to 50 years ago, but it is difficult to find magazines interested in them. I am wondering if editors think these are outdated and prefer something more modern.*

A. Current sports magazines do seem to favor more contemporary subjects. Get in the habit of studying current magazines for a better idea of the type of material they want. While there may not be a current market for articles on great football games—there may be a market for some of your material if you investigate a specific sports figure of these earlier days. Was he also a well-known businessman or prominent Lion or Rotarian? Perhaps there is a market among the fraternal magazines for such a piece.

Textbook Publishers

Q. *I would like to query textbook publishers with my ideas for textbook reader stories. Where can I find names of current publishers of textbook readers?*

A. Check listings for book publishers in WRITER'S MARKET. The librarian in your local school system may also be able to provide you with names.

19 Markets for the Same Idea?

Q. *I am puzzled by writers who claim that after mailing a piece 19 times and having it rejected, they mail it once more and sell it. Are they telling the truth? It seems that if a piece is slanted to a given magazine and it's rejected, there cannot be 19 other magazines with similar editorial needs.*

A. These writers *are* telling the truth, because they have carefully explored all possible allied market areas. For instance, a piece about Washington State fishing may not sell to other specialized sports magazines, but it might find a place in one of that state's Sunday supplements or in general men's magazines, fraternal order publications, etc. The number of markets a writer finds depends on his own resourcefulness and ability to revise, where necessary, to suit the new market.

Photo Markets

Q. *I am interested in a market for my photos. I am currently stationed in Asia in the service of the Army. I am equipped with a Pentax 35mm camera plus numerous auxiliary lenses and other equipment. I work in psychological warfare and civic actions, and through my job and contacts with the local people I have the chance to take many interesting pictures. I would appreciate any information you might be able to provide me concerning sales of, or a chance to show my work.*

A. There are hundreds of markets for photos you describe (either as single shots or a photo story) listed in PHOTOGRAPHER'S MARKET. The following wire services would also be good markets: AP Newsfeatures, 50 Rockefeller Plaza, New York City 10020 and United Press International, 220 E. 42nd St., New York City 10017.

Children's Series

Q. *I have a new idea for a series of children's books. How would I sell this series to a publisher? What are my rights? What are the usual rates and how do I state them?*

A. Query the publisher with an outline of the proposed series and sample chapters. The question of rights (such as book club, reprints, etc.) and rates would usually be negotiated by the writer or his agent with the publisher upon acceptance of the work and receipt of his contract terms. The usual royalties on a juvenile are ten to 15%, often split 50-50 with the illustrator. In some cases, where there are just a few illustrations, the illustrator is paid a flat fee and the author receives full royalty.

Humor Book

Q. *I have a book-length manuscript on wit and humor which is in the form of quips, jokes, doggerel, etc. What first step do you advise me to take?*

A. You might try to sell the manuscript to a book publisher. In your local library or bookshop, find some humor books and then query those publishers. Also consult the list of book publishers in WRITER'S MARKET. If you cannot sell this material in book form, you may want to sell small batches to magazines as fillers, or to cartoonists wanting gags. Check WRITER'S MARKET for these markets.

Sell Article Twice?

Q. *Is it unethical to cover similar material different ways for different types of magazines or does an editor automatically assume that information in an article is offered to him exclusively?*

A. It is common practice among nonfiction writers to get the most out of their research by slanting various aspects of their subject toward different markets. There has to be enough distinction between treatments, though, so the writer cannot be accused of selling the same story to two magazines.

Beginners' Markets

Q. *Do you have a listing of secondary markets where a neophyte can break in?*

A. Just because a magazine doesn't have a large circulation or pay much, doesn't mean its editor isn't as demanding about the material it uses. Hundreds of smaller circulation and low-pay publications are listed in WRITER'S MARKET.

Cookbook Market?

Q. *Is there any market for cookbooks from unknowns, on such subjects as menu planning and preparing easy meals or full-fledged dinner parties? How does a writer go about breaking into this field?*

A. There has been such an influx of cookbooks on today's market that any new one would probably need a specialized approach that hasn't been tried before. See if you can gather together recipes that relate to an appealing, unusual central theme. Send a query, including a brief outline, to book publishers listed in WRITER'S MARKET, who are interested in cookbooks.

Comedy Skits

Q. *I've written several short comedy skits. Could you tell me where to submit them, and how to go about it?*

A. Much would depend on the subject matter and the level of humor that is employed. There are various possible markets such as radio, TV, school productions, etc. If you think your skits could be used on TV, for example, you would have to submit them to specific TV entertainers through an agent. If the skits could be considered one-act plays suitable for school productions, you could send them to play publishers who specialize in this area. Check WRITER'S MARKET for listings of play publishers.

Truth or Fiction?

Q. *In general, is a story more salable if the publisher can present it as a true story rather than the same story fictionalized?*

A. This depends on whether the publisher is in the market for fiction or nonfiction. If he buys both, the writer must decide which category best suits his subject. There would not be any particular preference for a true story over a fictional one ... just a good one!

Heroes for Sale

Q. *"Write on familiar subjects," the novice is advised. I have written about real flesh-and-blood people, whose traits of character were admirable, and whom I felt were making noteworthy contributions to society. But where is there a market for such articles?*

A. Many newspapers run such profiles of interesting members of the community. Perhaps you could interest your local newspaper editor in the idea. There is also the possibility that these people you write about work for companies that have house publications, which could use such material. Then, too, their "contributions to society" might also suggest other specialized markets. (See WRITER'S MARKET listings).

Family Adventure

Q. *I sincerely believe my family and I have had more unusual incidents in our lives than most people, and I would like to gather these* *happenings, both funny and tragic, together in a story in third person, changing all names and places. I am undecided whether to start from my childhood or when I was about to enter the business world, using some anecdotes from my younger years in flashbacks. Would there be a market for a book of that type?*

A. Family adventure stories have been popular for a long time, i.e., *Swiss Family Robinson, Cheaper by the Dozen,* etc. There might be a market for yours too, but only if the story is exceptionally well written and offers incidents that have strong, universal appeal. Consider starting the story at a point of high interest in the leading character's life, then use flashbacks sparingly.

Get an Assignment

Q. *I have written a professional paper which may be published by a publication in my chosen field. My problem is that this publication pays only for material written on assignment. A friend told me, "Get the assignment." How do I get an assignment to do a paper that is already done?*

A. Assignments are the result of an editor's need to have a certain topic covered in print. Because he urgently wants such an article, he is willing to pay for it. He usually gives assignments only to established writers whose work he is familiar with and whom he knows he can rely on. Have you tried to find a publication in your particular field which *does* pay for freelance material? Check WRITER'S MARKET for payment rates. If you find that all the likely prospects are nonpaying, except on assignment, then choose one to whom you have not previously submitted your paper. Write this editor a lively, interesting query which will convince him of the need for such an article. Request that, if the editor deems the idea worthy of publication, you be given the assignment. Remember that since you are a stranger to him, you should show why you should be given the assignment. Include some pertinent autobiographical facts that clearly qualify you to write with authority on this subject. You might even provide a sample paragraph to give him an idea of the style and treatment you would use.

British Fiction

Q. *A recent letter from a writer friend mentioned that editors of magazines in Great Britain are receptive toward fiction in which the locale is in our early West and Southwest. Can you provide names and addresses of magazines that are published in Great Britain, particularly those that publish fiction? Also, what are postage rates and how about return postage?*

A. You'll find the information you want in *Writers' and Artists' Year Book* (The Writer) which lists a great variety of magazines published in England, Scotland, Australia and Ireland. Consult your local post office concerning postage rates and International Reply Coupons, to cover the return of your material from overseas.

The Comic Book Market

Q. *Will you tell me if comic books buy freelance material? What are the usual rates? The usual lengths? Is the story sent in regular manuscript form or is there a special form? Are there any books on the subject?*

A. Different comic book publishers have different policies concerning the purchase of material. Most of this material is written on assignment. The editorial staff determines current needs and then assigns a story to a writer and designates its length. One comic book publisher offers this helpful advice to would-be comic book writers: "Actual scripting of a comic book is a bit different from other types of writing, in that the medium is primarily a visual one. Movie scripting is perhaps the closest parallel. The writer of a comic must 'see' his action first, then fill in the visual gaps with verbal continuity. The greatest error, in my estimation, is redundancy in dialog or caption and illustration. To picture the hero as he crashes his fist into his antagonist's jaw and then place in caption, 'The hero crashes his fist into ... etc.' becomes a waste of effort. With only 32 pages to tell a story, each bit of space must be utilized to the fullest. Also, complete verbal description of a thing, a person or what-have-you is ill-spent effort, for the illustration can do this better. Unlike prose, comics stimulate the imagination both graphically and verbally. The idea is to move the reader in and out of the picture you have drawn, not to have the reader create his own pictures." A book that might prove useful is *The Comics,* by Coulton Waugh (Luna Press). For other books see the *Subject Guide to Books in Print* under "Comic Books, Strips, etc.—History and Criticism."

Stories on Record

Q. *For about a year, I had a program on a local station where I worked without scripts—just from notes. One day each week was devoted to children's stories, which were part fantasy but contained many facts about fishes. It seems to me this would be a painless way of introducing youngsters to the fascination of marine biology. Is there a potential market for material of this type? I have it all on tapes, and am afraid I do not have the attentiveness to detail and composition necessary to a good writer.*

A. Why not try querying some of the record companies that produce children's records? Or some of the companies now producing audio cassettes? Be sure to mention your radio program.

Prize-Winning Poem Marketable?

Q. *May a poem later be offered for sale to a magazine if it was entered in a prize contest and read over the radio, or if it received a prize, or if it was circulated in a mimeographed brochure that carried notice that the author retains all rights?*

A. Yes, such a poem may be submitted to professional markets, but some indication of its previous exposure should be included in a covering letter.

Shopping Guide

Q. *I've succeeded in interesting three local grocers in a weekly combination handbill and news-sheet which I will have mimeographed.*

If my grocer-sponsors agree, is there any reason why I can't legally accept paid ads from other noncompetitive local businesses? Also, my grocer-sponsors will be paying me for these sheets, but they will be offered free to patrons. Can I legally "lift" quotes from published material without bothering to get permission from author or publisher?

A. It would be permissible to accept paid ads, provided your grocer-sponsors have no objections. Regardless of whether your publication is offered free, however, you *must* get permission from the copyright owners to quote from published material, if it does not fall within the bounds of fair use. (See Chapter 33.)

Film Market for Animal Stories?

Q. *I am a professional storyteller via radio. I write my own children's stories and songs. My animal stories would lend themselves to film cartoons. Will you please advise me if there is an open market for this?*

A. Most film companies work through agents or on the basis of assignment. You might write a West Coast agent (see list in WRITER'S MARKET) about your radio credits, asking for his representation for your idea with a film company.

Publishing Poems

Q. *Is it wise to let a "little magazine" use poetry to get it into print or should I hold out for better markets? If I win a contest prize, will I retain the right to sell the same work?*

A. "Holding out" can be a frustrating game. There is a prestige and satisfaction in being published by the "little magazines," so don't be afraid to try them—if they are copyrighted. If they are not, your poem's publication will place it in the public domain and you will have to write a new version to obtain a copyright, or copyright your work yourself at a ten-dollar expense. Usually contests permit the contestant to retain all rights to his work, but it is best to check the rules in each case.

Fictional Confession?

Q. *Should a confession story be completely true, or can it be fictional? Should the byline be a pen name?*

A. The important thing about a confession story is that it *could* happen, not that it did. Most confessions do not give bylines, so it is unnecessary to be concerned about pen names. Only the editors know who the authors are ... and they don't tell the readers! For more information, see the *Confession Writer's Handbook,* by Florence K. Palmer (Writer's Digest Books).

Downbeat Story Market?

Q. *I have written a story about a woman's emotional disintegration as various pressures upon her reach the point where she can no longer cope with them. It does not end happily. A recent editorial comment said, "... it's a little too grim to be entirely satisfactory to us." I believe this attitude toward an unhappy ending is shared by all women's magazines. And this is definitely a woman's story; it is not a confession. I am discouraged, not by rejections per se, but by the apparent lack of markets for this kind of story. Are there any suggestions in your excellent bag of tricks?*

A. If the caliber of your writing is high, you could try the quality markets, such as *Atlantic, Harper's,* etc. Bear in mind, though, that your story must have something to say to readers above and beyond the mere chronicling of one woman's misfortunes. It must in some way deepen readers' insight through its larger view of life.

Foreign Markets

Q. *Is it true that foreign publishers disdain the cover letters that so many American writers enclose with their manuscripts?*

A. We are not aware of any foreign aversion to cover letters unless it is to the over-long, redundant or "chatty" type of letter that U.S. publishers would be hostile to also.

Juvenile Book Reprint?

Q. *Would it be possible for me to have my juvenile book, now out of print, published as a reprint edition? If so, which publishers could I contact regarding same?*

A. You might query publishers of reprints in the juvenile field, such as Scholastic Magazines, Inc., 50 W. 44th St., New York City, 10036. For additional listings, please consult WRITER'S MARKET.

Children's Sayings

Q. *Do you know any magazine which would be interested in some very funny sayings of children which I have collected from children I have known?*

A. For submission of individual funny sayings, try *Reader's Digest.* If you could incorporate these sayings into a humorous feature article, this might be material for women's magazines. Check WRITER'S MARKET for more information.

Advertising Slogans

Q. *Can you offer any suggestions regarding how to sell original mottos, slogans, etc. for advertising?*

A. Selling original mottos and slogans for advertising is a very difficult job, since many national advertisers automatically reject any idea submissions of this type from individuals because they are afraid of plagiarism suits. A few freelancers have been successful in placing advertising slogans with local advertising agencies who are handling a local client's work. For your slogan ideas for nationally-distributed products, consult the *Standard Directory of Advertisers.* Companies are listed in this book by products. By selecting a company, you could then find from the listing which advertising agency is currently handling their account. Then you could write the advertising agency to find out whether they would be willing to look at your ideas and, if usable, pay you for them.

Special Market

Q. *Do you know if any manufacturer of aluminum publishes a magazine that might be interested in freelance work connected with the aluminum industry?*

A. According to the latest edition of *Gebbie's House Magazine Directory,* both Aluminum Co. of America and Reynolds Metal Co. buy some freelance material related to their industry. Alcoa's address is 1501 Alcoa Bldg., Pittsburgh PA 15219. Reynolds' is Reynolds Metals Bldg., Richmond, VA 23218. See also listings for trade journals in WRITER'S MARKET.

Sell Ideas?

Q. *Is there a market for ideas for scripts and stories and possibly films? I have several ideas for science fiction pieces, but feel I am not in a position to expand them into salable pieces.*

A. TV producers, picture producers, and magazine editors will look at completed scripts, not simply ideas. In addition, TV producers require that material be submitted through agents and will not look at material submitted directly by the writer. Perhaps you have a friend who is a good writer, but short on ideas, with whom you could collaborate.

Church School Papers

Q. *I am interested in doing some writing for church school papers and magazines. Where can I find lists of these markets?*

A. See listings for religious publications in WRITER'S MARKET.

Submitting Strip Ideas

Q. *In collaboration with a local commercial artist, I am developing an idea for a daily comic strip. We hope to have some material to offer soon. Could you send me information concerning the size of drawings, the number of episodes which should be submitted, and other requirements made by syndicates to whom we expect to submit our work?*

A. Milton Caniff, creator of *Steve Canyon,* suggests submitting 12 to 18 daily strips, entirely finished. For Sunday strips—at least two. One Sunday sample should be reduced to newspaper size by means of a matte photo print and hand colored to simulate the finished product as it would appear in the paper. (Caniff prefers to do his strip originals in a 6-7/8" x 21-5/8" size for the dailies and 17" x 23-1/8" for the Sunday strip.)

Sell TV Commercials?

Q. *I often get ideas for various commercials, but how can I go about getting a start in this field? Can commercials be written freelance, or does each company hire their own staff of writers?*

A. Yes, most companies have their own advertising departments as well as advertising agencies to prepare their commercials. It is, therefore, very difficult for a freelancer to submit material and have it accepted. The few writers who have been successful in this way have concentrated on companies in their immediate area, calling on the advertising manager of the company to present the idea.

When to Submit?

Q. *Can you give me any general information about the lead time required for submitting stories to quarterly publications? At the mo-*

ment I am interested in submitting a Christmas story to a religious magazine which is a quarterly.

A. A Christmas story for a quarterly publication should be submitted six to nine months in advance. Check with each editor for his preference.

Jokes for Sale

Q. *Where can I find markets for jokes?*

A. The markets for jokes are several: magazines; disc jockeys on radio stations; comedians who work in night clubs and on television. The magazine joke markets are all listed in WRITER'S MARKET. Gags for disc jockeys can be submitted to them directly with SASE for return. Jokes submitted to night club comics are usually submitted to them in care of the club where they are performing. TV comedians depend almost entirely on staff writers, so there is not much of a freelance market for jokes for them.

Agent for Poetry?

Q. *I am a poet who needs a literary agent. I wonder if you could help me find a reputable one who would work with me on agreeable terms.*

A. There is such a small market for poetry that almost no agent will handle someone whose sole output is poetry. Most poets attempt to sell their poems individually to magazines, hoping eventually to be able to present enough published credits to a book publisher to interest him in publishing an anthology of their work. If by "literary agent," you really meant literary critic, and would like to have an evaluation of your poetry by a professional, several firms offer this service for a fee, and advertise in magazines for writers.

Selling a Column

Q. *What books do you suggest that will help a writer in becoming a columnist—a chatty one, nothing serious. I have written several articles, but don't know whether to take them to a local editor. I don't know how to prepare them.*

A. You might refer to a Writer's Digest book, *The Creative Writer,* edited by Aron Mathieu, which has a comprehensive chapter, "How to Syndicate Your Own Column."

Book Reviews

Q. *Does one have to be an editor, or need special training in order to write book reviews? I have often felt, after reading a book that I could write concise, descriptive and honest opinions.*

A. No, one does not need special training in order to write book reviews. If you can write interesting, brief reviews of a book that an editor wants to publish, that's all that matters. When contacting book review editors to see if they could use your work, enclose a sample book review you have written on a relatively new book.

Starting Out

Q. *About book reviewing—how does one go about breaking into this field? I have worked in a library and have sold a few of my juvenile stories.*

A. Try submitting a book review to your local newspaper or to some of the smaller magazines (religious or women's) that print reviews. Inform them of your sales in the juvenile field and ask them if they would like to use your services. Remember, though, that most local newspapers and small magazines do not pay for reviews—except with the book itself.

Payment for Reviews?

Q. *As a freelance book reviewer, I have published work in several newspapers. From submission to publication, I have waited from two weeks to two months and have always been paid after publication. With my last three reviews, however, I have been waiting for three to six months without publication or payment. In each case, I asked to review a specific book, and the book editor sent the book. I read the books, researched and wrote the reviews. I expected, from payment I'd received before, to receive a total of $130 for the reviews. Are these newspapers obligated to pay me for the reviews which they assigned to me and which I did as competently as any other reviews I've done? If I am stuck with only the review books for "payment," I shall leave book reviews to people who don't need the money.*

A. Since so few newspapers pay for book reviews—beyond the book and the byline—you were lucky to have collected cash from the previous reviews. Newspaper editors are not geared to working with freelancers, and under daily pressures rarely respond to letters of inquiry. The fact that you asked to review a certain book and the editor sent you the book doesn't necessarily mean he "assigned" the review to you and is legally obligated to use/pay for it. He sends out many books on request, and depending on space and the reviews, decides what to publish.

Selling Gags

Q. *I have, over a period of time, gathered together about 75,000 jokes and anecdotes covering American life from 1870 through today. Many of the sources were books and items which are out of print. I have written more of my own gags as well. I would like to start a service furnishing gags or jokes to cartoonists at two dollars each—they select the topic they desire and I come up with the number of items they want under that topic. I have the gags under all headings. A separate file would be maintained for each customer, so they would have only the jokes or anecdotes they purchased. Will you give me any ideas about how to start this service, to help cartoonists with good material and help me with part-time work?*

A. There are several ways you might sell some of the gags. Check a copy of WRITER'S MARKET at your public library reference department. Its gag and humor markets category lists cartoonists and agencies that purchase gags from people like you. The listings tell what kind of material they're looking for, subject matter, payment rates, and how to submit. You might also contact the Cartoonists Guild, Inc., 156 West 72nd St., New York City 10023. Ron Wolin is executive director. Or write to Gag Re-Cap Publications, Box 86, East Meadow, New York 11554, which offers a highly useful means of checking the originality of gags, trends in the publishing industry, addresses of markets in need of material, and payment rates. An additional source is George Q. Lewis, Executive Director, National Association of Gagwriters, 74 Pullman Ave., Elberon, New Jersey 07740, for information about services for gagwriters.

How to Submit Clippings

Q. *What are clippings? How do I know what kind an editor will buy? What is the best way to submit them? How much money can I earn from sending clippings to markets?*

A. Clippings are newspaper items of possible interest to trade magazine editors. If the editor buys clippings, they should be related to his magazine's subject matter and readership. Paste them on an 8-1/2x11 sheet of white paper, and put your name and address in the upper left-hand corner, with title of the newspaper (or other source) and the issue date directly underneath the clipping. For the most comprehensive list of magazines that buy clippings, see WRITER'S MARKET. While you can earn some small payments for clippings, don't expect this to be a sizable monthly income—unless you have access to a great many different newspapers and magazines from which you can obtain your clippings at no cost to you. It's important to remember that you should only send to an editor the specific kinds of clippings he requests. General mass mailings of clippings to editors will be a waste of your time and postage. Follow the editor's submission requirements. Some prefer no SASE, since, due to the large volume of clippings received, they are unable to acknowledge or return unused clippings.

Greeting Cards

Q. *I'd like to write for the greeting card market. Is there a book or other publication that will give me a better idea of how to write for greeting cards and how and where to sell them? Other than going to greeting card shops and stores with greeting card display racks, how can I learn what's being marketed today in the field?*

A. See *The Greeting Card Writer's Handbook,* edited by H. Joseph Chadwick (Writer's Digest Books). This book contains market information as well as how-to information on writing every kind of greeting card. Greeting card market information is updated annually, and it's possible to buy the updated market list from *WD* when it's available each year, usually in the fall. Another publication that will be helpful is *Greetings Magazine,* the business magazine of greeting cards, stationery, gifts and allied products. They have an excellent annual edition which gives factual, informative and interesting information about the greeting card and gift industry, including details on merchandising and promotion. Write *Greetings Magazine,* 95 Madison Ave., New York City 10016, for additional information.

Greeting Card Idea

Q. *I understand that greeting card companies purchase "ideas" as well as original verse. Would a suggestion that they use a poem by a well-known author come under the classification of an "idea"? The poem I have in mind was written in the 16th century so there would be no copyright problem.*

A. Yes, your suggestion could be considered an "idea."

Editorial Market?

Q. *I am particularly interested in writing editorials. Any information will be appreciated.*

A. Unfortunately, there isn't much of a market for editorials, since most newspapers have their own staff writers who prepare the editorial page. You could contact newspaper editors in your immediate area, sending a few sample editorials. Also see the "Op-Ed" markets published in WRITER'S DIGEST from time to time.

Puzzle Markets

Q. *I would like some information regarding the marketing of crossword puzzles. I have made a few which are now in varying stages of completion. All mine are 15x15, though I do have a few 21x21. I have written four syndicates concerning crossword puzzles; one syndicate said they were well stocked, thanks anyway; another said they did not use crossword puzzles and the other two didn't even have the courtesy to answer my letter.*

A. Magazines buying puzzles are listed in WRITER'S MARKET. Magazines using puzzles usually want them aimed toward their specific audience, so it's usually a matter of creating a puzzle to fit a specific magazine rather than creating some puzzles and then trying to sell them. There are, of course, crossword puzzle magazines themselves and their names and addresses are also listed in WRITER'S MARKET.

Humor for Sale

Q. *We have written material we feel is humorous. We are interested in finding a market for this material, which is written in the form of comic dialog. If you could send us any helpful information, we would appreciate it. We are particularly interested in finding an agent who could market it for us.*

A. No agent is interested in handling a client who writes humorous material unless the writers have already attained a certain amount of success on their own. Most beginning comedy writers try to write specific comedy material for either night club comedians in their area or speakers at club gatherings, etc.

Markets for Speeches?

Q. *I once saw a request for someone to do research for other writers, someone who could write speeches for women's clubs, etc. Will you steer me in the right direction to locate and obtain such a job?*

A. As far as writing speeches for women's clubs is concerned—if a specific woman who is an officer of a club requires a speech to be written for her, you would have to find this out on a local level, of course, and make your contact to sell your services directly. The same would hold true for local businessmen or politicians who need speech writers. Writers who need researchers would probably advertise in writers' magazines, so watch the classified ads there.

Easiest? Best? It Depends

Q. *Who or what is the best market? Or most easily salable, for that matter?*

A. There is no such thing as one best market since so much depends on the type of writing each individual writer does. A market is good for a particular writer if he writes the kind of material that market needs. In general there are more markets for articles than short stories.

Film Scripts

Q. *In writing for film production companies, am I correct in thinking they are the ones who do the actual filming, not the script writer? Are scripts prepared like TV scripts?*

A. Yes, the film production companies do the actual filming and scripts are prepared like TV scripts. These film production companies, however, are not preparing films for exhibition in regular movie theaters as you probably know. Their films are "non-theatrical" and specifically designed for industrial public relations use.

Monologues for Children

Q. *Please list names and addresses of a few editors who would be interested in monologues for children.*

A. About the only publishers who buy monologues for children are the religious houses who publish Sunday school materials. Check the religious, and juvenile and teen listings in WRITER'S MARKET.

Recommend an Agent

Q. *Please recommend an agent in the New York area. I am going to be 73-years-old next November. My greatest ambition in life is to have this book published. I don't feel that I have the energy to trot around to publishing offices. I am too old.*

A. All of the agents listed in WRITER'S MARKET are thoroughly reputable and we would recommend any of them. Many agents, of course, are not willing to work with previously unpublished writers so you may have to write a number of them before you are able to find one that is interested in handling your work strictly on a commission basis. Why not try marketing your book yourself? Mail it to the publisher of your choice, always being sure to enclose sufficient return postage.

Humorous Monologues

Q. *Who buys humorous monologues?*

A. It depends on what the subject matter is and who the potential audience is. If, for example, your material is the type a night club comic could use in his routine—he's your market. If it's light, frothy material of the type that would appeal to a women's club—they're your market. A monologue implies a spoken delivery so there aren't many published markets for this type of material. If by humorous monologue you really mean short prose humor—these markets are scattered throughout WRITER'S MARKET.

Agent?

Q. *Walt Disney Productions states that they look at original scripts only if submitted by an accredited agent. They list no agent's name, so how do I go about finding their agents? Could you give me this information? I have several children's stories, two of which would make excellent cartoon movies. Would the same agent handle both types of stories? I have heard that an agent sometimes asks for a fee in advance. If this is true, how much is the accepted fee, and what is his total fee? Is it percentage of sales?*

A. A list of agents with details on types of material they handle appears in WRITER'S MARKET. The agent tries to market your work and handles the business arrangement. You have to provide him with stories he can sell, of course. Some agents do not charge a reading fee, but they usually will not work with previously unpublished or unproduced writers. Other agents do charge reading fees.

Sell Poems?

Q. *I was wondering if you would help me get my poems published in a magazine, since publishing a book would probably be out of the question.*

A. It is almost impossible these days to get a book of poems published unless you are an extremely well-known and nationally-recognized poet. There are many magazine markets for poetry, however, and they are all included in WRITER'S MARKET. Submit your poems, one to a page, with your name and address in the upper left-hand corner. Be sure to SASE.

35. Submitting Manuscripts

Fold or Flat?

Q. *I have read that manuscripts under 12 pages may be mailed folded in thirds. Is this true?*

A. It is customary to fold only manuscripts that are under five pages. Anything over this should be mailed flat.

Cover Letter?

Q. *I have submitted to various publishers in the juvenile field and find it more difficult to write the cover letter than the manuscript itself. To date I have not had anything published except newspaper articles, so I do not include any credits in my cover letter. I understand it should be short—but how short?*

A. It's not necessary to submit a cover letter with a manuscript. If your article or story is completely written in the proper form, it can be submitted with SASE and no cover letter. If you wish to include a cover letter anyway, all it would have to say would be "Dear Editor: Here's an article (or short story) I think might interest your readers because (and then tell why). May I have a report from you on it within 30 days? Thank you."

To Glue or Not?

Q. *In an issue of* WRITER'S DIGEST, *the fiction editor of a well-known magazine was quoted as pleading with writers to affix, rather than attach, return postage on the return envelope. Yet, I've had professional instruction to attach it. What to do?*

A. This is one editor who prefers to take a licking! Some editors feel it saves valuable time in their offices. There is also less danger of losing the stamps when they're pasted onto the return envelope.

Resubmitting

Q. *One of my stories was published in an amateur magazine. (I received no money.) May I send it now to another magazine for money?*

A. Yes, but there are several things to keep in mind. First, if the magazine was not copyrighted, your material is now in the public domain and anyone could have reused it as is. To submit it now to a magazine and get it copyrighted as part of the magazine, it would have to be revised sufficiently to be considered a new work by the Copyright Office. If the magazine in which it originally appeared *was* copyrighted, you'd have to clear with the editor whether they acquired only first rights or "all rights" to the material.

Poetry Book

Q. *I am submitting a volume of poetry for consideration in a contest open to those who have not yet published a complete volume. What procedures should be followed for the inclusion of poetry previously published? Does it suffice to list the magazines in which they appeared, or must permission be sought for each poem?*

A. If this contest involves the eventual publishing of the winning poetry books and if your poems originally appeared in copyrighted publications, you must secure permission before the book's publication.

Mailing Carton

Q. *Will you give me the address of a supplier of carton containers for the purpose of mailing book manuscripts?*

A. Some of these firms advertise in the classified pages of WRITER'S DIGEST. See the latest issue for current names and addresses.

Tearsheets

Q. *In freelancing, it is often necessary to submit a tearsheet or sample of some previously published work. How are these usually obtained?*

A. Publishers frequently furnish free tearsheets on request. If these are not available, you may offer to buy copies of the issue either from the publisher or from back-issue magazine dealers. Xerox copies may be made on machines in most large libraries, but these are not as desirable as actual sample pages.

Multiple Editor?

Q. *When submitting to an editor who edits one or more related magazines, should one submit to each magazine separately or to the editor? Also, I recently sold a story to a Sunday school paper to which I do not have access. Would it be proper to write them to send me copies when it is published?*

A. Send your manuscript to the editor in care of whichever magazine is your first choice. If he finds it more suited to another of his magazines, he will consider it accordingly. It *is* permissible to write the publisher, tactfully requesting the publication date and a copy of the issue in which your story appears. Many publishers automatically send out complimentary copies on publication.

How to Submit Poetry

Q. *Must poetry always be double-spaced? Length requirements are given in numbers of lines. Does the number of lines, then, replace the usual word count? Or should both be given? How does one arrange the manuscript for a book of verse? One poem to a page? If illustrations are offered, how should the page for which they are intended be indicated? What are the established minimum or maximum length requirements for the book of verse? Is it wise to combine humorous and inspirational verse in a single volume?*

A. Longer poetry, usually more than three stanzas, may be single-spaced. It is not necessary to include a word count—only a line count. Prepare the manuscript with one poem to a page, in the order you prefer. And insert the illustrations, also one to a page, where you would like them in the printed version. In view of your two different themes, it might be helpful to divide the volume into two sections, with appropriate headings for both the inspirational and humorous segments. There are no strict rules about length, but it would be a good idea to have at least 20 poems.

Return Postage on Books?

Q. *Should return postage be enclosed with book-length manuscripts? I've never done this, and manuscripts have been returned without any request for postage.*

A. You have been fortunate to encounter publishers kind enough to assume this cost! Sufficient return postage should definitely be clipped to the letter you enclose or to the first page of your manuscript.

Picture Book

Q. *I recently submitted a manuscript of a child's picture book to a book critic. He said it was excellent and could make no suggestions for improvement, and that in its "final" form, it should sell. I had* *the story typed the same as a fiction manuscript. Is there a special form for picture books?*

A. Picture book manuscripts are often submitted with only one or two sentences per page, the way they might appear when accompanied by illustrations in the printed book. To be on the safe side, why don't you ask that book critic what he meant by "final form"?

Male Confession Writer?

Q. *Does a male writer, writing as a female, have a chance in the confession markets? Is it true that some of these publications require an affidavit attesting to the truth of the story?*

A. Since confessions do not carry bylines, men have just as good a chance as women in this field, provided they can write convincingly from a female viewpoint. If a confession seems "true" to readers, that's all that counts; affidavits aren't necessary.

Christmas Ideas

Q. *I always have such good Christmas ideas when the Christmas issues come out. When should these ideas be sent?*

A. Submit your Christmas ideas six to eight months in advance of the season.

Do Credits Help?

Q. *I have finally made a short story sale. Should I indicate this sale on the first page of my manuscripts to insure more careful consideration?*

A. Since most editors prefer to judge a fiction manuscript solely on its own merit, it is better not to try to impress them with a list of credits. A record of past sales won't increase the chances of a good story or make a poor one sound any better.

Counting Words

Q. *How do I count the number of words in a manuscript? Must it be sent flat or can it be folded?*

A. Every word counts. The word "a" counts as one word. Abbreviated words count as one word. Count the exact number of words on three representative pages, and from the average number of words per page compute the number of words in the manuscript. In a longer script, of say 50 pages, you should count exactly the number of words on five pages and compute the total from that. Indicate the approximate number of words (2,700 not 2,693) in the upper right-hand corner of page one of your manuscript. Manuscripts under five pages can be folded in thirds, but longer manuscripts should be sent flat

Missing Manuscript

Q. *What does a writer do if his manuscript never comes back? Can I make a duplicate copy and send it to another publisher?*

A. Inform the magazine to which you've sent your manuscript that you are officially withdrawing it from their consideration. You may then send your story elsewhere, but be sure you type a new original and retain the carbon copy of both your letter and the new manuscript.

Free Contributions

Q. *Would editors accept free contributions from the authors? Or would this be infringing on some freelance writer who has to be paid in order to live? My reason for asking this is because I would like to see some of my material published, material for which I do not feel I should accept money to have it reach the public. It is moralistic writing and carries a message. What say you?*

A. There are some magazines that do not offer any payment for contributions. If it is the magazine's policy to pay for the material they use, however, you should not offer them your contribution free. Do not be misled into thinking that just because it's free, an editor will use it. If, in the editor's estimation, it's worthy of being printed, he will gladly pay for it (and you can send the check to your favorite charity). If it doesn't seem publishable to him, then the fact that it's free will not persuade him that it should be used.

Multiple Query?

Q. *Is it permissible to submit a query covering the same article to two different editors at the same time? Sometimes the time element is important and if one editor delays answering, it could be too late to query another.*

A. It is permissible, but not always practical, to submit the same article idea to several magazines simultaneously. Most writers abhor the long delay it takes to get an answer from a magazine editor, but realize on the other hand, that if they do make simultaneous submissions to editors they are going to face the possible situation of more than one editor asking to see the article and having to be told that someone else is considering it. Naturally, an editor who is told that he will have to wait in line is not going to look very kindly on the next letter from that particular writer. In the case of article ideas which are timely, many freelance writers use this technique: they point out in the letter to the editor that it is an extremely timely query and request a reply in a certain number of days. Most editors would respect this request.

Submitting a Book

Q. *What are the special angles a writer should watch in submitting his finished book to a publisher?*

A. Keep a carbon. If your manuscript is lost, regardless of whether you sent it registered mail, the publisher will not pay for retyping. Do *not* bind or staple the pages. Enclose return postage. Type your name and address on the title page and your name only on each succeeding page in the upper left-hand corner. What you have to say belongs in the book. Any matter enclosed in a covering letter that is not specifically important cannot help you, and might hurt. In a covering letter belongs a list of your previously published works only if of some importance, and issued by a respected publisher, as well as information regarding documentary evidence to support any facts in the book that might be questioned.

Quoting Copyrighted Material

Q. *I want to quote a couple paragraphs of copyrighted material in a novel. Am I required to obtain permission to quote before submitting the book, or is this the responsibility of the publisher who accepts the work?*

A. When submitting your novel manuscript to a publisher, you should include a page indicating the source of the original copyrighted material you used, so he can request permission to use it if it remains in the final version of the novel he accepts for publication. Some publishers, however, require that the authors obtain permissions after the book has been accepted.

Mailing Query Letters

Q. *What do you suggest for mailing queries: a ten-inch envelope with a six-incher for the return, or an 11" envelope with a ten-incher for the return?*

A. The 11" envelope with a ten-incher return would probably have a neater appearance, especially since the editor may return other material along with his answer.

Fillers

Q. *What are the rules on submitting identical fillers to the 150 to 200 word $1 to $2.50 markets?*

A. As long as the markets are noncompetitive in either subject matter or geography, you can submit fillers to more than one market at a time.

Foreign Market

Q. *What procedure does one follow for submitting manuscripts to publishers abroad? The difficulty seems to be in getting them back again at a reasonable rate of postage. Is there any cheaper method than the International Reply Coupon which I understand is limited to first class?*

A. The International Reply Coupon is the most convenient method of handling the return postage but some countries also have special rates for manuscripts. Inquire about specific countries at your local post office.

Simultaneous Submission

Q. *A playwright I know sends seven copies of his plays simultaneously to various producers. He claims it is all right to do the same with fiction and nonfiction. If two editors make offers, then you can take the best offer, or even bargain, he says. Is it all right to do this without telling the editor it is a simultaneous submission?*

A. Your friend is playing with fire. Unless a magazine is known to accept simultaneous submissions (and there are some), it would be best to submit fiction or nonfiction to just one editor at a time. Many editors won't read a manuscript they know another editor is considering. And if they *don't* know it and happen to be the loser in a two-editor interest, they're not likely ever to read *another* manuscript submitted by that writer.

Withdraw Manuscript?

Q. *If a magazine refuses to return a story or article after many months and refuses to reply to inquiries, is it proper to send a regis-*

*tered letter informing the editor that as of a certain date you intend
to submit the material to other publications? Or are you at the mer-
cy of the guilty magazine?*

A. Yes, the right thing to do is to send a certified letter informing
the editor that as of a certain date, you intend to submit your material to other publications.

Double Submissions

Q. *Is it a good or bad practice to submit more than one short story
manuscript to one editor at a time?*

A. Though it means more waiting, it is advisable to submit only one
short story manuscript at a time. If the first is accepted, the editor
will be happy to receive another one from you at a later date. If the
first is rejected, its weaknesses, fresh in the editor's mind, may inadvertently minimize the merits of the second which is read
immediately after the first.

Submitting a Book

Q. *Should a book manuscript be submitted in a box and not a
home-sewn binding or clip-board spring cover? Does this mean that
the manuscript should be submitted with individual loose pages? Is it
preferable to submit the original copy of the manuscript, or will a
carbon copy work just as well?*

A. The individual pages should be loose in the box in which you are
submitting a book manuscript. Editors prefer this to having to hold
a bulky, bound manuscript to read. It is preferable to submit the
original copy and many publishers will not even read a carbon.

Mailing Book Manuscripts

Q. *Please let us know what you think of sending book-length manuscripts in "jiffy bags," and enclosing correct return postage.*

A. It's a "novel" idea, but a cardboard box is still the safest way to pack manuscripts to prevent corners from bending, etc.

Selling Plays

Q. *I am in need of information concerning requirements for play submission—whether sales are made on a cash or royalty basis, information about rights, and a list of reputable agents. Also needed is information on the Dramatists Guild contract that says the author can demand his living expense away from home or on tour while participating in production. Does this pertain to previously unproduced authors or just members of the Guild?*

A. Plays for the legitimate theater are handled through a dramatic agent. See WRITER'S MARKET for a list of agents. Payments are made on a royalty basis usually with an advance payment to the author before the play opens. For complete details on the Dramatists Guild and their contracts, write Dramatists Guild, 234 W. 44th St., New York City 10036. Plays are copyrighted by sending two copies of the play and ten dollars to the Register of Copyrights, Library of Congress, Washington, D.C. 20559.

Submitting Plays

Q. *Do all plays—one-act or full-length plays—have to be bound regardless of whether they are sent to a play publisher, producer or little theater? Some contest rules state they read only "bound" plays.*

A. Very short plays can be submitted as loose pages held only by a paperclip. The request for "bound" plays means only that they should be submitted in a flexible binder, available in a stationery store.

Reprint Submissions

Q. *How do I indicate on my manuscript that my articles have been previously published?*

A. In the upper right-hand corner of your first page, indicate "Second Rights" as well as the name and date of the publication in which this material first appeared.

Multiple Consideration

Q. *How can I submit a manuscript to a firm when I want to have it considered for all their publications?*

A. Send the manuscript directly to the publisher instead of the individual magazines. The publisher's name and address can usually be found next to the copyright notice at the beginning of the magazine. The editors can then decide which, if any, of their publications might be able to use the manuscript.

Gag Submissions

Q. *What is the standard way to submit gags to cartoonists?*

A. On a 3x5 card or paper slip, neatly type a description of the scene and caption. Stamp your name and address either on the front or back of this slip, and also specify a code number in an upper corner. This number plus your initials would be placed on the back of the cartoonist's rough, to identify the gagwriter. Mail the gag slip (keeping a carbon copy for yourself) in a 3½x6½ envelope and include a folded return envelope of the same size.

How Much Personal Background?

Q. *I'm a beginning writer, but I don't think I have to scream that fact to an editor. How much information is necessary for inclusion with a manuscript? Also, what do editors think of short manuscripts sent folded in half in 6½x9½ envelopes?*

A. The only personal information necessary is your name and address in the upper left-hand corner of your manuscript. The manuscript folded in half in a 6½x9½ envelope is satisfactory, but be sure to SASE for return.

Illustrations for Books

Q. *What is the standard format for preparing illustrations for juvenile books? Also, is material considered more salable to juvenile publishers if accompanied by illustrations?*

A. Publishers of juvenile books prefer manuscripts not accompanied by illustrations, since they prefer to work directly with freelance artists who know their requirements. There is no "standard format," though illustration board and opaque watercolors are frequently used.

Canadian Writers

Q. *Do Canadians stand an equal chance in the American market with people who live in the United States? How can one best manage return postage?*

A. Yes, Canadians stand an equal chance in the American market, provided they are sending material that is competitive with what American writers can supply. Many Canadians solve the return postage problem by sending a check for the correct amount, plus the Canadian exchange to the postmaster of the nearest large American city, requesting that he send them a number of American stamps, which they can then paste on their return envelopes. International Reply Coupons (available at your post office) for the amount of postage may also be enclosed rather than stamps.

Controversial Article

Q. *Among several articles I hope to write is one of a very controversial nature. Even if an editor thinks the piece is interesting, he will likely want to be very sure of the authenticity of the source material—especially since I'm an unknown writer. How do I proceed?*

A. Most writers of controversial articles maintain a detailed list of their sources of information and have this ready for presentation to an editor who questions the author on any specific point. Send your article or query and advise the editor you'll be glad to provide verification on any points.

Series of Novels

Q. *Is it proper to indicate in a cover letter that my novel is the first of a series? Also, may the publisher who accepted a portion of a series turn down any succeeding books in that series? Would it be ethical to submit these to another publisher?*

A. Indicate the proposed series, but do it in an initial query. Don't send the complete manuscript unless the publisher asks for it. Check WRITER'S MARKET for submission requirements. It is doubtful that the series could be divided among different publishers, but if you change the characters' names and make no references to events in previous books, there's no reason why these books couldn't be marketed on a separate basis without any tie-in with the series.

Booklength Manuscript

Q. *In mailing a book manuscript (often too large and unwieldly to be accommodated by even the largest manilas) how should one best prepare it to insure safe arrival? What provisions should be made for its return?*

A. It is best to ship a bulky book manuscript in a stationery box. Send manuscripts at the special fourth class book rate, with "Return Postage Guaranteed" under your name and return address on the package. Be sure to enclose return postage, and always keep carbon copies of all work mailed.

Submitting Greeting Card Verse

Q. *What is meant by "identifying marks" on poems sent to greeting card firms?*

A. Since such poems often do not have titles, it is a good idea to number them (one poem to a page), and keep carbon copies with the corresponding numbers for your own records. When the editor sends payment for one poem from a group, he can refer to it by number.

36. The Business of Writing

Writer's Attorney

Q. *How would I go about finding a competent copyright and literary rights attorney?*

A. Most of these are concentrated in the major media centers, such as New York, Chicago and Los Angeles. In about 200 cities throughout the country there are services which will refer you to a qualified lawyer. Such services are sponsored by the local bar associations. If there is one in your area, you'll find it listed in the yellow pages of the telephone book under "Lawyer's Referral Service." If there's no listing, call your local bar association. The service referring you to a lawyer does not usually charge a fee, but most likely there will be a consultation fee for a half-hour discussion with the lawyer.

Writer's Guild

Q. *How can a writer qualify to become a member of the Writer's Guild?*

A. This organization for professional writers has two branches—one in the East and one in the West. The Mississippi River is the dividing line. The Eastern branch consists of freelance TV writers or staff newswriters for radio and TV networks; the Western branch includes these and also screen writers. You must have sold or been employed to write a TV, radio, or movie script within two years prior to your application. The initiation fee is $300. Membership dues are ten dollars per quarter (West), $12.50 (East) applied against one percent (West) and one and one-half percent (East) of a writer's earnings in WGA fields.

Fraudulent Royalty Statement

Q. *Is it true that some book publishers cheat the artist with false royalty statements?*

A. Such defrauding is rare. Most writers accept the statements of publishers in good faith. Many publishers take the precaution of protecting themselves *and* the writer through the following clause in the standard Society of Authors' Representatives book contract: "The Author or his duly authorized representatives shall have the right upon written request to examine the books of account of the Publisher insofar as they relate to the work; such examination shall be at the cost of the Author unless errors of accounting amounting to five (5%) percent or more of the total sum paid to the Author shall be found to his disadvantage, in which case the cost shall be borne to the Publisher."

Pay Your Interviewee?

Q. *When you interview a person (not famous) for a feature-type article (human interest) do you agree to pay him for this opportunity? Or do you agree to pay a certain percentage of the check when it is sold? Is it customary to pay them at all?*

A. In such a situation, the interviewee would normally not be paid at all. If the interviewee indicates he will expect payment on publication of the article (an expectation that's possible but not too probable), you must use your own judgment in determining beforehand whether you wish to do the article under these circumstances and how much of a percentage you will be willing to pay. There are no set fees for this.

What's a Fiction Bestseller Worth?

Q. *Would you tell me how much a book on the fiction bestseller list would bring an author if it were number one for a period of a week or a month? Assume the book sells at average price and a standard royalty is paid.*

A. The standard minimum royalty payment on trade books is: ten percent of the retail price of the book on the first 5,000 copies, 12½% on the next 5,000 and 15% thereafter. Prices paid for movie paperback and book club rights vary, but a novel that sells 45,000 hardcover copies and is bought by movies, book clubs and paperback houses could earn the author more than $250,000.

Dead and Gone?

Q. *How does a writer protect himself from magazines that suddenly die, leaving him holding the bag for articles published, but not paid for, or the problem of manuscripts that will never be returned? It's happened twice since January and the magazines still hold three of my stories. Is there any way to force return of manuscripts and irreplaceable photos?*

A. If he can't locate the publisher, the author doesn't have much recourse when a magazine folds. Some publications make the conscientious effort to return material they've been holding, but others simply disappear. You could try writing the postmaster or Better Business Bureau in the city where they were located to see if you could obtain the current address of the former owners. Remember, you should always keep a carbon and, if possible, negatives of photos so that additional prints can be made, in case of loss.

Time Limit in Contract

Q. *I sold an original story and screenplay almost a year ago. Since the time the contract was signed and my work was taken, the producer has not been in touch with me. He hasn't paid me a nickel so* *far. According to the contract, he has to pay only when they start the principal photography, or when the production money is banked. Since there is no time limit in the contract, I wonder if there is any law that protects me? What can I do if the producer is unable to raise sufficient money for the production?*

A. Unless you had a time limit written into the contract you signed, (which is always advisable) you do not have much choice except to wait for his ability to obtain production money. On the other hand, if he has had to abandon the project, he should return the material to you. It is up to you to contact him to see what can be worked out.

Comedy Fees?

Q. *An entertainer asked me to show him a few of my skits, which run 15 minutes to a half hour. How much should I charge for permitting him to use the material?*

A. What you should charge for your material depends largely on how much you can get. Minor entertainers obviously cannot pay big fees, while big-name entertainers pay their writers large salaries. You might want to ask the National Association of Gagwriters, (74 Pullman Ave., Elberon, New Jersey 07740) this question, since some of their members also write comedy material for performance.

Fair Fee?

Q. *I have been requested to write the life story of a woman who has given me reason to believe she has had unusual experiences that would be worthwhile book material. She feels that since she will relate the episodes and I will write them into an interesting biography, I will be a hired person, somewhat in the capacity of a stenographer, and paid on that basis. I feel that my talent is worth a contract that will guarantee me a 40/60 percentage of the book rights and a percentage on the same basis if the book proves to have other market values. I would like your suggestions on drawing up a contract that would treat both of us fairly.*

A. Most freelance writers consider that their talent in writing a book for a subject is worth at least a 50/50 split of the payments. My suggestion is that you draw up a contract detailing what you think is fair to yourself (and the subject) and secure a signature on this agreement before you proceed with any work.

Newspaper Rates

Q. *I would enjoy writing freelance articles for the local, small newspapers, but I'm in doubt about the pay received for such material. What is the customary pay for varying lengths of articles?*

A. Payment for work contributed to local newspapers is usually by the published inch and it varies from newspaper to newspaper. A typical Midwest daily of 300,000 circulation, pays 50¢ a column inch and smaller papers pay less.

Trade Magazine Writers

Q. *Is there a national association of trade writers?*

A. Yes, there is a national association of trade magazine writers. It's called Associated Business Writers of America, and their mailing address is P.O. Box 135, Monmouth Junction, New Jersey 08852.

Fulltime Freelance

Q. *For many years I've "suffered" with a deep-seated desire to write. But, I guess I've been too lazy to sit down and get started. Finally, I've come to my senses and decided to "give in." That's why I'm writing you. How does a person get started? How does he "break into" the field and make enough to support a family? Perhaps I'm looking for a miracle. The dull routine of the business world is beginning to irritate me. There isn't even very much money in it. Any help or encouragement you can offer will be greatly appreciated.*

A. I'm afraid if you think there isn't much money in the business world, you will be disappointed too, in how little remuneration there is for the beginning freelancer *until* he develops his talent and marketing ability. There are hundreds of fulltime freelancers, however, who started small and did freelance writing on the side while holding a regular job until they reached the point where they could support themselves and a family on their writing alone. The best place to start, of course, is with articles, since the market for them is much greater than short stories, and there is article material all around every person in every town. Trade journals are a good place to start.

Can an Unknown Sell?

Q. *I am a beginner trying to sell juvenile stories and articles. Five months have passed and no sale. Is the juvenile field overcrowded? Would personal letterheads and envelopes help me break through for a first sale? Does it go against my chances to sell because I have never sold?*

A. A personal letterhead is not going to influence the sale of a juvenile story or article. A manuscript has to sell itself. You mentioned that you've been trying for five months, but you didn't mention how many submissions that represented. Have you really analyzed your work in light of the type of material these magazine editors are publishing? Can it stand up? If you think your work is good and is marketable—don't give up. Good luck!

Reprint Sales

Q. *Would you explain how "digest" magazines pay for articles they reprint from other magazines? What percentage does the original publisher get, and what percentage goes to the author? If the author has sold first rights only to the original publisher, does he receive the entire reprint amount? Should he try to sell a reprint of his article to a digest magazine, or do digest editors read most publications and make their own selections?*

A. In the digest reprint market, payments vary. Some pay 50% to the original publisher and 50% to the author. Others pay the publisher or the author—depending on who owns reprint rights. *Digest* editors *do* make many of their own selections, but don't let that stop you from submitting. When you sell reprint rights to publications you are entitled to the entire reprint fee. But the original publisher does, in effect, hold other rights in trust for you, even if he has bought first rights only, until you write and ask that the rights be returned to you.

Ghost?

Q. *Could you send me the address of a ghost writer in New York City?*

A. A number of persons offer this type of service for a fee and you'll find their names and addresses in the Manhattan Yellow Pages under "Writers." Ghostwriters can also be found in advertisements in WRITER'S DIGEST. It would be best to write each one and find out what they would charge to work with you.

Deductible?

Q. *In regard to permissible income tax deductions for writers, can I deduct the cost of: editorial service prior to submission of a manuscript to a publisher; rent and upkeep of a study; stationery, postage, and supplies? A query on the above was made to the local IRS prior to including these as deductions on my tax return. After I advised the party at the tax office I had two manuscripts submitted to market through an agent, but none of my work had yet been published, he advised me that I could claim these expenses. Based on this, I included these deductions in my return, and received the following notice from the IRS: "Your claims for expenses must be capitalized and later deducted over the life of your copyrights." This does not seem right, and there appears to be some confusion, even with the IRS personnel, on the correct interpretation of the tax law in this regard.*

A. There are three categories under which a writer may be classified for Federal income tax purposes depending upon the extent of his writing activity. The deductibility of expenses depends upon the category in which the writer is classified.

The three categories are as follows:

1. If writing is a generally full-time activity engaged in for a livelihood, it will qualify as a "trade or business."

2. If the writer writes only part-time and his writing produces a profit for two out of five years it will be presumed for tax purposes to be an activity engaged in for profit.

3. The not-for-profit writer.

If a writer's activity constitutes a "trade or business," he will normally deduct items such as stationery, postage and supplies from gross income as ordinary and necessary business expenses. Expenses such as rent and upkeep of a study are covered by the new "home-office" rules adopted in 1975, and are deductible only if the study is used *exclusively and on a regular basis* as a regular place of business, and the deduction may not exceed the writer's gross income derived from his writing business. Editorial services may be deductible for magazine sales, or may have to be capitalized and depreciated when the manuscript for which they were incurred will have a useful life of more than one year — such as a book.

If the writer is engaged in writing for a profit, but not as a "trade or business," under the "home-office" rules he normally will not be able to deduct rent and upkeep of a study since it would not be considered a place of business for tax purposes. Editorial service is again deducted or capitalized depending on the useful life of the manuscript, and stationery, postage and supplies are deductible from *adjusted* gross income, as distinguished from gross income.

For the writer not engaged in writing for a profit, rent and upkeep of a study is usually not deductible. Stationery, postage and supplies are deductible only to the extent of the writer's gross income from the writing activity, and any excess is deductible against future income from writing activity, if and when received. Editorial service expenses are again deductible or capitalized depending upon the useful life of the product, but these deductions are also limited to the writer's income from writing, and may be limited to income from the specific work for which the expense was incurred.

Press Credentials

Q. *How does a freelance writer (with no official credentials) get a press card, or admittance to sections marked "Press Only"? Our baseball club has been granted a major league franchise but will be playing in the old ball park until the new park is built. Is there any way I can get into the "Press Only" room to take pictures and get personal interviews from the players without lowering myself by rope from above? Or is this one of those situations when a freelance writer is left out in the cold?*

A. You should get an advance assignment from some specific magazine or newspaper to do a feature on the baseball club players. You could then present this letter of assignment to the public relations director of the baseball club and gain admittance through him to the players' area. There are no official credentials as such that the freelance writer can use. He usually has to ally himself with some specific newspaper, magazine or syndicate market to obtain entry to these otherwise restricted quarters.

Press Cards?

Q. *Last week, I visited a company to research some information I need in order to finish a project. Their behavior was very harsh. They said they would not give any information to anybody unless he had credentials proving he is a writer. The same thing happened when I did research work at a museum and at a medical research laboratory. Reporters, telephone operators, merchant seamen, detectives, private investigators and even photographers have identification cards. Why not writers? Our job is just as important as theirs! I am sure that the rest of my colleagues feel as I do. Why don't we have a writers association to bring together all those interested in the writing field and provide them with the backing, support and benefits of a powerful, nonprofit, internationally-recognized organization?*

A. There are many freelance writers organizations already in existence—and they are designed to meet the needs of specific groups of writers—National Association of Science Writers, Inc., American Society of Journalists & Authors, Inc., etc. A list of such organizations, with addresses, appears in the *Encyclopedia of Associations* in your public library.

Business Cards

Q. *Having finally gotten a toe in the door with sales to national magazines and California newspapers, I would like to have business cards printed identifying me as a freelance writer. This would probably simplify introducing myself to people I wish to interview or ask for information. Can you suggest the best wording for such a card?*

A. Keep the card as simple as possible, with clear, tasteful lettering. For example, in the center you may have your name and directly beneath it, the words, "Freelance Writer." In the lower left-hand corner, in smaller print, include your address ... and in the lower right, your phone number.

Fair Price?

Q. *What do you consider a fair price for writing the historical articles to be published in a commemorative book marking the 100th anniversary of a village? As a freelancer I've sold news and features to the* Evening Bulletin.

A. Remuneration will have to be based on two factors: 1. What you think the job is worth and 2. What the customer will pay. You will simply have to calculate approximately how much time and effort will be spent on researching and writing these articles, estimate the budget of your client, then charge accordingly.

Who's the Author?

Q. *If a writer buys a plot from an advertised source, or if a writer pays for extensive help in plotting his story or novel, is the finished product legally and ethically his own?*

A. In both cases, the finished product belongs to the purchaser who has actually produced the written manuscript, even though he has used the help of others. When there has been extensive help on your novel, you could, if you wish, include an acknowledgment in the foreword or preface.

Sell Ideas?

Q. *I would like to know if there is a market in selling ideas to established writers. I have what I feel is a powerful plot for a "what-if" novel of the* Seven Days in May *genre, but I don't have the Washington political background to make it authentic. Is it possible to sell such an idea to a known writer who has written books with a Washington background? If there is such a market, what is the usual procedure in presentation and payment? Are there any agencies that arrange collaboration between writers?*

A. There aren't any agencies that arrange collaboration between writers and unfortunately more people are in the position that you're in—having an idea but not the background to write the book. Those people who do have the background also have plenty of ideas and aren't in need of such collaboration. Usually, the only way this type of collaboration works is if you can find an expert in your local area with whom you could negotiate.

37. Using a Pen Name

Anonymous Author?

Q. *Can a writer use a pen name, become successful or even famous, and still remain anonymous? This person dislikes publicity, and is very shy with persons outside her family and friends' circle. What in your opinion would be the advantages and disadvantages of anonymity in such a case?*

A. With the publisher's help, a writer could achieve both success and anonymity. The chief advantage of this would be the fulfillment of the author's desire to remain unidentified. The disadvantages would include lack of public acclaim and the thrill of seeing one's own name on the book. Other disadvantages would include the necessity to reject all interviews and photos, and worst of all, the burden of having to keep a secret.

Pen Name Location

Q. *If a writer uses a pseudonym, does he place it or his real name at the top left-hand corner of each page of his manuscript?*

A. The real name is usually used in the upper left-hand corner of each page to identify the creator of the manuscript. Put your pen name on the title page as a byline, i.e., "The Eye of the Beholder" by John Doe.

Check Cashing

Q. *Sometimes an author writes under a pen name because he doesn't want his real name known. How does the writer cash a check made out to his pen name—especially if he's well known in a small town?*

A. When the manuscript is submitted under a pen name, the author usually includes his real name and address on the title page, so that the check will be made out to him and he can cash it without letting anyone know what the check is for. If, on the other hand, the check is made out to the pen name, then the author can simply endorse it with the pen name, then endorse it over to his own real name and cash it that way.

Pen Name Protection

Q. *Please tell me how I can write an article under a nom de plume and yet be able to prove in event of a court case that I wrote it. I know that I could register it in the copyright office under my real name and the nom de plume, but I would prefer just to copyright it and register it under my pen name. The article is not going to be published by a magazine—it's a private effort, but I don't want to lose my rights when it's printed and circulated. This leaves me with the problem of having to prove that the pen name is really me. Could I mail a copy of the article to myself with both names on it and keep it unopened in a safe place—as proof? Could I send a copy to a banker or lawyer or someone? I think some plays in England are handled in this way. What would you suggest?*

A. Writing an article under a pen name and mailing one copy of it to yourself with both your pen name and your real name included might work. Or you could get the copy, with both names on it, notarized. Most writers who are going to use pen names usually notify their postmaster and banker that they will be receiving mail and, hopefully, checks in that business name. Keep in mind that in the United States, if you privately print an article and distribute it—unless you get a copyright on it and print the copyright notice on it before distribution—you are otherwise placing your article in the public domain.

Danger!

Q. *Because I hope to begin my political writing where George Orwell (Eric Blair) concluded his career, I would like to adopt the pen name, George Orwell II. Will I need permission from his heirs?*

A. Yes, you would need permission, but I doubt that Mr. Orwell's heirs would allow you to cash in on his reputation. Try to make it on your own!

Pen Name

Q. *I am a patrolman on the Memphis Police Department, and since my stories often deal with policemen, I must for obvious reasons use a pen name. When submitting short fiction, is it desirable to include a short letter requesting the use of your pen name? Or would the cover sheet be used for this purpose? If I ever do sell anything, I would like to be able to cash my check.*

A. In the upper left-hand corner of your manuscript's first page, type your name and address, and your pen name in parentheses. Use this pen name as the byline under the title, too. No letter is necessary.

Several Names?

Q. *I love western adventure and have the rough outline of three western stories, but it doesn't follow that a fat woman of 40 years would have much appeal to western story fans. In other words, they look for a book by a man, as I do myself. Also, I feel I need different names for the different types of material I write. I wish to adopt a pen name for my western stories, and perhaps a shortened form of my own name for science fiction, and gothic mysteries.*

A. Send a list of names in which you might be receiving either mail or checks to both your bank and postmaster, so material will be safely delivered to you. The procedure on manuscripts is this: type your legal name and address in the upper left-hand corner of the first page of the manuscript; underneath the title of your story, type the word, "by," and then list the pen name you prefer to use for that particular story.

Already In Use?

Q. *I would like to use a pen name but how can I be sure the name I select isn't one that is already being used by someone else?*

A. Except in cases where extremely well-known names, such as Ann Landers might be registered as a trademark, most writers simply go to the Library of Congress Catalog card index in their public library, look up the last name they want to use, and see if anybody else has already copyrighted books in that name. Your librarian could assist you in locating the directories of Library of Congress Catalog authors.

Value?

Q. *What is the real value of the pen name? Is it customarily used among professional writers today?*

A. A pen name is used to protect the identify of the writer employing it. Of course, there are any number of reasons why a writer wouldn't want his real name associated with the material he writes. There might be a college professor of mathematics who secretly authors who-done-its and doesn't want the word to get around to his students and colleagues. Or the writer's family might object to his career and, to disassociate himself from them, he changes his name. Or the writer might simply dislike his real name—it may be hard to pronounce or look unwieldly in print—so he adopts a more suitable one. For most writers, though, there is sufficient satisfaction in seeing one's own real name in a byline.

Adopt a Real Name?

Q. *I want to use as a pen name a lovely name which happens to belong to a little girl in England, an occasional pen pal of my daughter. Must I ask permission? What if I were to pick a name out of a telephone directory?*

A. Yes, it would be best to ask permission of the little girl in England (or her parents) if you plan to use her name as a pen name in America. It's not a good idea to pick a name out of a telephone directory. A better idea is to choose a combination of two different names.

38. Legal Problems of Writers

Same Title?

Q. *The title of a short story that is currently appearing in a magazine is the exact title I wish to use for my first novel. Could there be any complications in such a situation if my novel were published under the same title?*

A. Since titles alone can't be copyrighted, the similarity should not cause any trouble.

Actual Company Names

Q. *Can a writer legally use the actual name of a business firm in fiction when it doesn't reflect uncomplimentarily on the business?*

A. Well-known companies such as Macy's or Marshall Field & Co. would not look unfavorably on a little free advertising imbedded in a nationally distributed piece of fiction, provided such usage is strictly for purposes of atmosphere and realism. Nothing even remotely illegal or distasteful should be connected with the company name. For example, if your story deals with a criminal who dupes a department store, you'd be on safer ground if you used a fictitious company name, to avoid the possible impression that the real store is not smart enough to escape being duped. As a rough rule of thumb, when in doubt, fictionalize.

Invasion of Privacy?

Q. *A neighbor of mine, who is disfigured from the hips down, is a recluse. I have built an interesting story around such a woman, saying she became this way because of an auto accident at which time her lover was killed. (She had been about to be married.) I slander her in no way, yet my husband feels I will have a lawsuit on my hands if the story gets published. I would appreciate any advice.*

A. It would be best to change as many of the obvious true-to-life facts as possible to avoid an invasion of privacy suit. Give your heroine a different age, size, hair coloring, nationality, etc. Add new mannerisms, idiosyncrasies and other aspects of personality. Use a totally different setting if you can. After all, the only basic idea you need is that of a disfigured recluse. It is not necessary to make the type of disfigurement identical to that of your neighbor. Use your creative imagination to produce a completely new individual based on the general idea but not the exact details of your neighbor's life. In fact, you might even experiment with the idea of making the leading character a man instead of a woman.

Ownership After Death

Q. *My brother and I worked together on his manuscript. He asked me to help rewrite, edit and type his work. When he passed away, all the manuscripts he had were packed into a box and given to me. I have found some I am sure will sell with some rewriting and corrections. I would like to submit these for publication using both our given names and the last name. What are my legal rights? Will it be necessary to ask permission from his other heirs, and would I have to share any profits with them? These papers were an outright gift.*

A. If these manuscripts were willed to you, then they are your possession and you may try to get them published without asking the permission of the other heirs. If there is any doubt about the legality of this "gift," it would be best to consult an attorney.

Information on Libel

Q. *For about a year I have been collecting material for a critique of a psychosomatic therapy and panacea of all that troubles man and the world. The head of this well-organized metaphysical school is known to sue for libel any who dare criticize his teachings. What should I do?*

A. We're not able to offer you expert legal advice. This can come only from a paid attorney. The book, *Say It Safely: Legal Limits in Publishing, Radio & Television,* by Paul P. Ashley (University of Washington Press) would be helpful.

Deductions

Q. *I have a problem that probably is common to aspiring professional writers. Are there any publications that offer information regarding the writer and IRS? The reason for the question is simple; my recent return was audited and my expenses as a writer (second source of income) were questioned. I was told deductions would be allowed only for the amount of income, with costs beyond that amount not being deductible.*

A. See the answer above under the question "Deductible?" as it applies to the part-time writer-for-profit.

Using Real Names

Q. *Is it permissible, in a book of personal experiences, to use real names and to relate real episodes without obtaining written permission from the persons mentioned? Or do you recommend that both characters and events be fictionalized?*

A. It's always advisable to change the names of real persons and the locale of real episodes, to avoid suits for invasion of privacy by the parties concerned. Even if your copy is nothing but complimentary, the individual sometimes resents being placed in the public spotlight and goes to court to prove his point. This, of course, refers to a *book* of personal experiences, since a book will give the person much more exposure, and the episode that is being related would be much lengthier also.

39. In the Public Domain

Book of Poems

Q. *You have given me the idea that my verses, which appear in a weekly uncopyrighted newspaper, are now in public domain. In order to incorporate them in a book of poems later, would I have to make changes in each one?*

A. Yes, if you want to copyright your book, you'll have to produce a new version of the work, since you cannot secure a copyright for something that is already in the public domain.

Erroneous Phrase

Q. *Some periodicals indicate "Buys all rights. Publication not copyrighted." If a periodical is not copyrighted, it seems the only rights it can claim are the rights to first publication. Am I right?*

A. The publisher of an uncopyrighted publication may say "all rights" on his check, but the lack of copyright will permit anyone to make whatever further use of the material he wishes.

Government Hearings

Q. *While writing an article that requires extensive research, I discovered a book containing quotes—that would be a great addition to* *my research—from doctors and scientists testifying before a Senate committee. Would this quoted material be in the public domain? In using this material, need I give credit to the book or its author? Is my knowledge of the facts now sufficient for making statements or paraphrasing the speakers?*

A. If the committee was an open hearing, the material is in the public domain and free for you to use. Obtain a report of the hearing to be sure that material quoted is indeed from the hearing and not from interviews conducted by the author of this book. If you paraphrased and used limited material, you would probably be safe under the fair use section of the Copyright Law, as long as you give credit to the book, author, and publisher in your article. Extensive quotes, however, would require you obtain permission.

What's "Publication"?

Q. *Each year our writers' club holds contests in several divisions: short story, article, and various types of poetry. First, second, and third place winners, as well as honorable mentions, are announced in the published and unpublished divisions. As the procedure now stands, no method exists for exposing the winners' entries to the view of the league membership. We would like to start a creative magazine with subscription limited to club members, or a yearbook with the same type of limited subscription. Objections concern copyright. Some members fear that such exposure of material would in effect place the material in the public domain; or that a first rights sale to a paying magazine would be jeopardized.*

A. The only way your contest entries could be made available to members is to copyright them and then print them separately or in a magazine, sending them out by direct mail. Whether circulation to league members only would jeopardize the sale to a paying magazine would have to be tested. Certainly unless you *do* copyright this material, printing it even by mimeograph or multilith with a subscription method of distribution would put it in the public domain.

Quoting From Newspapers

Q. *Can I quote personalities whose statements were included in daily newspapers and columns? Where can permission to quote be obtained? From the author? From the newspaper? Or from the columnist? I collect inspirational sayings and want to publish this material in a book.*

A. Since news cannot be copyrighted, if you are using quotations that are in *news* stories about personalities, you would not have to request permission. (I am assuming that the quotations were accurately recorded by reporters and they were not of a nature that the personality would subsequently sue for inaccuracy.) Many newspaper features and columns, however, are covered by copyright and you would not be able to lift quotations from these without requesting permission from the newspaper or the syndicate first.

Government Publications

Q. *Is it permissible to quote directly from a document issued by the United States Government Printing Office? I have never been able to discover whether that material is copyrighted, or how credit should be given. Many of the leaflets would be very useful incorporated in articles or books, or as research for an article. Do our taxes which pay for printing these items give us right to appropriate the words?*

A. Yes, materials published by the government are in the public domain. There are a few minor exceptions—some connected with the post office and some exceptions in which copyrighted material is inserted in an uncopyrighted public domain Government Bulletin. Such material would be accompanied by the printed copyright notice. If you have any doubts about whether a specific leaflet you want to use is copyrighted or not, it is best to write the issuing government agency for clarification.

Poem in an Uncopyrighted Magazine

Q. *Does having a poem published in an uncopyrighted magazine entitle it to be reprinted without author's knowledge or consent?*

A. Unfortunately, once the material appears without copyright notice, it falls into the public domain and anyone may make whatever use of it he wishes. This would include reprinting it without notifying the author in any way.

Rewrite Government Publications?

Q. *May a writer rewrite a government publication or article and offer it for sale as long as he credits the source?*

A. Almost all United States Government publications are in the public domain, so articles and information can be rewritten and used again for sale, as long as credit is given the original source.

Facts in Public Domain?

Q. *Are "facts," such as those found in medical journals and reports, in the public domain? Scientific literature, the way I understand it, is in the public domain and can be used by other writers. Is this true?*

A. Most medical journals are copyrighted, so material in them would not be in the public domain. "Facts" as such cannot be copyrighted, however, so if there are well-established findings quoted in a number of medical journals that could therefore be called "facts," you could work them into your articles without the original researchers' consent. You can't lift written copy verbatim, of course, but the information—the "fact"—can be included in your writing.

Poems in Newspapers

Q. *Recently our weekly newspaper started a poetry corner and invited contributions of poems. I've contributed several and enjoyed seeing them in print. A friend tells me I've lost all rights to the poems I've sent in to the newspaper, though. Would I be able to sell them to a magazine? I hate to lose the poems, as I might want to put them in a book someday.*

A. If the newspaper in which your poems appeared is not copyrighted (and most of them aren't) then your poems are now in the public domain and can be used by anyone, including you—if you want to submit them to other markets. You might be able to sell them to a magazine but the copyright of the magazine would not cover your particular poems since they are still in the public domain. And you must notify the magazine your poems are in the public domain. If you assembled them later into a book, those particular poems are not covered by the copyright on the book. The only way this material can be copyrighted in the future is if you revise it.

40. Rights and Responsibilities

Rights Question

Q. *What is the difference between first North American rights and first serial rights when submitting to a major magazine?*

A. Both phrases are usually taken to mean the same thing, namely the right to publish the material once for the first time. The word "serial" refers to newspapers, magazines, etc., that are published on a continuing basis. First North American serial rights covers first publication rights in both the United States and Canada, and American magazines that distribute in Canada usually want this extra protection.

Defunct Magazine

Q. *I sold a short story to a magazine which is now defunct. Who owns the story now? Can I submit it to a reprint magazine?*

A. The publisher who bought the story owns it for as long as his copyright is valid. Your right to submit it to a reprint magazine would depend on what rights you originally sold.

Rights to Fiction Characters?

Q. *Does the character and the name of the character belong to the copyright owner or the story itself?*

A. It is customary for the character to belong to the copyright owner. There is a notable court case involving Dashiell Hammett's selling of motion picture rights in *The Maltese Falcon* to Warner Brothers. After this sale, Hammett then granted CBS the right to use Sam Spade, the leading character in *The Maltese Falcon*. Warner Brothers sued but lost. Since then, movie companies make their contracts more specific about rights to certain characters as well as their stories and titles. You, as the author, might specify your wish to retain the rights to your characters.

Subsidiary Rights

Q. *What rights do I sell on my book?*

A. It is logical to offer "book rights only," but, if you are a beginner, you are in a tough bargaining position regarding the terms in your book contract for movie, syndicate, paperback and book club rights. Try to retain as many of these rights as possible. It is recommended that the author's share of subsidiary rights should be *no less* than 75% on foreign editions, 50% on paperback and book club sales and 90% on TV and movie sales.

Revise vs. Original?

Q. *About five years ago, I sold a children's story to a magazine that greatly altered and shortened it. It was published with a credit line that said, "adapted from a story by Joseph P. Ritz." There is no question the magazine owns the publication rights to the story as it was published. But does it also own the rights to the original manuscript, to date unpublished?*

A. The story the magazine paid for was your original one, which they then changed as they saw fit. Sorry, but this story no longer seems to belong to you unless, by agreement with the publisher, you retained certain rights to it. If you're not sure, write the original publisher.

Quoting Lyrics

Q. *In my story it would help add realism to use the titles of a few popular songs, and some "snatches" of the lyrics (as being played by the orchestra or coming from the juke box). Would it be necessary to get permission or give credit for this use?*

A. If you're going to quote directly from the lyrics, you will definitely need the music publisher's permission. A list of publishers of popular songs appears in a directory (availible in most public libraries) called *Variety Music Cavalcade*.

Trade Names

Q. *In a short story I've just completed, I have used the trade names Zyglo and Magnaflux, which are the property of the Magnaflux Corporation. The reference is used only to give authenticity to the lead character, who is a factory worker. There is nothing derogatory connected with it. Am I legally required to secure permission from the company to make such a reference?*

A. There should be no objection to your fair use of these trade names, but it wouldn't hurt to drop a note to the companies involved, anyway.

They're Yours for the Taking

Q. *Recently I wrote a short story as an assignment for a correspondence course I'm taking. When the assignment came back, a number of specific word changes were suggested. Can I legally use the wording suggested by the instructor in these instances?*

A. Feel free to appropriate revisions of correspondence course instructors. They lay no claim to any word changes made as part of the teaching process.

New Title?

Q. *Having read an article in a small magazine that I did not ap-prove of, I would like to answer with an article of my own in a newspaper. Would it be permissible to use the same title for my new article or should I use a new title and mention the old one some-where through the article?*

A. By all means create your own new title, and if you wish, mention the other one in·the body of your article.

Exposé Problems

Q. *I am in the process of writing an exposé-type book. Since the materials I plan to expose are copyrighted, obviously I cannot quote from them without permission of the authors. I doubt that any au-thor would consent to my using his material to prove a point against himself. How do I go about doing this legally?*

A. Remember that copyright protects only the exact wording of a passage. One way of accomplishing your goal without needing per-mission might be to paraphrase those authors' remarks, using foot-notes to indicate their source.

"All" Rights

Q. *What does "buys all rights" mean? Does it mean they buy first and subsequent rights? Or that they buy any rights offered?*

A. "Buys all rights" means they buy the rights to *all* possible ave-nues of sale on that manuscript—such as book, movie, TV, etc. Some publications that buy all rights, however, will reassign rights to the author after publication. Check this point with the editor.

Photocopy?

Q. *Most books now carry the legend: "No part of this book may be reproduced or utilized in any form or by any means, electronic or mechanical, including photocopying, recording or by any information, storage and retrieval system, without permission in writing from the Publisher." Does this mean that a writer, with access to a Xerox is not allowed to reproduce a page or portion thereof for his private research file without first getting the permission of the publisher?*

A. If the reproduction of a text is just for your own private research file, it would be all right to use the copier the same as it would be to copy the facts in longhand. If any of your manuscripts submitted for publication are going to use a verbatim quote from such material, you would need permission.

Rights

Q. *Will typing First North American Rights on a manuscript still assure the author of retaining all other rights? If an editor's acceptance check is stamped "All Rights" after you have specifically offered to sell him only first rights, can you write, returning the check, and object without jeopardizing the sale?*

A. In addition to specifying on the manuscript the rights you are offering for sale, you may also include a note in which you clearly indicate the rights you wish to retain. If the acceptance check is stamped *All Rights* and you object, you may return the check with a tactful letter in which you outline the rights you prefer not to sell. Of course, there is always the chance this may jeopardize the sale (especially if purchasing all rights is the publisher's established policy), but if you are strongly opposed to yielding all rights, then this is a risk you'll have to take. Publishers can be reasonable, though, and you might be able to make a special arrangement concerning the assignment of rights. But this should be done prior to endorsing the acceptance check.

Cookbook Problems

Q. *I am compiling a specialty cookbook. Some recipes are original, others have been gathered from various publications. Is it necessary to list the source of each recipe, or may I just call it a collection of recipes? If I change the amount of an ingredient or add a new ingredient, may I call it an original recipe? On this type of manuscript, would editors rather have a query alone or a query accompanied by an outline?*

A. If you are quoting the recipes verbatim from copyrighted publications you will need permission. A change in ingredients and new description of procedures would make it a new recipe, although not an original one. A query and outline would be preferable when submitting to a book publisher.

"Best" Rights?

Q. *What are usually the best rights and/or most profitable rights offered by writers of short stories and books?*

A. Most magazines list in publications like WRITER'S DIGEST and WRITER'S MARKET the rights they buy on short stories. If they don't indicate a specific type of rights, the writer should list in the upper right-hand corner of the first page of his manuscript "First North American Serial Rights Only." This gives the magazine the privilege of printing the story once with all other rights remaining with the author. As far as books are concerned, this arrangement is individual with each book and author, but for recommended book royalty and subsidiary rights percentages, check the index to this book.

Poem Rights

Q. *I have been sending an article each week to a newspaper in which I use a poem (not composed by me) along with Bible scripture and a few words of my own. Am I allowed to use this poem?*

A. If these poems come from books, for example, whose copyright is still in effect, you will definitely need permission to quote them.

Permission to Quote?

Q. *In writing an article, is it legal to quote from the sources occasionally and give credit in a footnote or is it necessary to get the permission of each author or publisher the writer quotes?*

A. If the quotes are short enough, they would come under the copyright principles of fair use, and no permission would be needed. The footnotes would be a good idea.

"Rights" Problems

Q. *Is it necessary to write for permission from each publication that has published my poems, in order to compile a book of poetry from my published work? Some indicated they bought first rights only. Does this automatically give permission to sell or publish again? And if some were first published under pen names, must they be republished under the same name or can they be published under my own name?*

A. If you sold only first rights, then you own book rights, but they are held in trust for you by the original publisher and he must be contacted. If there are some instances where you're not sure what rights were purchased, you'd better check with the publisher. Though written originally under pen names, the poems may now be presented under your own name. Your projected book should contain a list of acknowledgments, indicating where these poems first appeared.

What Rights?

Q. *While most "how to" books advocate specifying rights for sale on manuscripts, one popular seller claims this is a mark of amateurs* *and that editors who buy other than what is offered might reject for this alone rather than dicker over rights. What is the accepted practice?*

A. It is customary and businesslike to offer First Serial Rights unless the magazine's editorial listing in WRITER'S MARKET states it only buys all rights. Then the writer has to decide whether he wants to sell under those terms.

Rights Infringement

Q. *Since ideas can't be copyrighted, would it be necessary to obtain permission from the author of a short story before expanding the material to book length?*

A. You are not at liberty to base a book on another author's short story without the consent of that author, since he has the exclusive right of adaptation of his own work.

Rights Unknown

Q. *Eleven years ago I sold a juvenile story to a now defunct children's magazine. In their acceptance letter, they did not mention the rights they were buying and I cannot remember what I signed on the back of the check. Since I understand now that children's stories can also be sold as books, how may I find out what rights I have?*

A. You should try to locate, through the Copyright Office, the last known address of the copyright owner and check with him on the ownership of book rights. But first it might be helpful for you to secure the free government circular No. R22, which deals with such searches. Address: Copyright Office, Library of Congress, Washington, D.C. 20559.

Foreign Copyright

Q. *I am curious to know if a word-for-word translation of any foreign language book without the publisher's consent is considered plagiarism?*

A. If the foreign language book is copyrighted and copyright has not expired, it may *not* be translated without the consent of the copyright owner.

Definition

Q. *What is meant by "rights"? What rights are you supposed to sell?*

A. A writer is entitled to decide who shall own the right to print his story for the first time or reprint it or make it into a movie, etc. Such rights are his protection against those who would come along and freely use his work for their own purposes. The rights most commonly offered for sale are first North American serial rights, which mean the writer is selling the right to be first to print this particular work one time. All other rights still belong to the writer. On the manuscript, in the upper right-hand corner of the title page, indicate the rights you are offering for sale.

Title Rights?

Q. *Nine years ago I sent a manuscript to a publishing firm. They rejected (as did others) after keeping it so long it was necessary to write them about it. Now I read they are publishing a book by that exact title. The title is extremely important to my book. Do they have all the rights in this case?*

A. A title cannot be copyrighted, but it *can* be protected under rules that prohibit unfair competition, which would prevent a publisher from bringing out a book with a title that's the same as a recent bestseller. Actually, there's nothing stopping you from keeping your title, especially if your story is completely different from the published one with that title.

Adapting Classics

Q. *I am interested in adapting stories by other authors for TV. How can I determine whether this material is in the public domain?*

A. Before January 1, 1978, copyright protection under the old law of 1906 was for 28 years and could be renewed just once for another 28 years. Any copyrighted material over 56-years-old (except for material whose copyright expired from 1962 to 1977, and was renewed by Congress while it considered a new Copyright Bill) would now be in the public domain. Under the new law, copyright is for the author's life plus 50 years.

Too Much!

Q. *After reading a novel by a famous author, I decided to write a continuation of that novel. Of course, I will have to use the author's characters, and to hold the same atmosphere, I will have to describe them as he did—same habits, speech, etc. Also, because of the characters recalling their past, I will have to use some of the author's situations and his characters' dialog. Do you feel that I would be asking permission for too much?*

A. If the original work is still under copyright protection, then indeed you would be asking permission for too much.

Permission Problem

Q. *I wrote a sonnet inspired by a columnist, and wonder now if I must get permission from him to submit it for publication. The first line of the sonnet contains the first seven words of the column, and the poem expresses some of his ideas in my words.*

A. While it's all right to use the prose as inspiration for your sonnet, you should secure permission to quote those first seven words of his column.

Rewrite Tennyson?

Q. *Recently, I rewrote a poem of Alfred Lord Tennyson's, using only a few of his original stanzas, and took the viewpoint of the woman rather than the man he had written about. Can this sort of thing be published? If so, what type market would consider it?*

A. Lord Tennyson's work is in the public domain, so you are free to write your own version of that poem. Since you do not indicate which poem it is, or whether your version is an amusing parody or a serious poem, it is difficult to suggest markets. But since appreciation of your poem would probably depend on the reader's familiarity with the original, some of the quality literary or quarterly magazines would be possibilities.

Copyright Question

Q. *I have an old book that has lost its cover and first 144 pages. I have no way of knowing the author, publisher or date. It contains very specific accounts of Indian battles, giving dates and names of the chiefs and settlers involved. Could I offer these tales to a publisher? How would one find a publisher of this early Americana?*

A. Write the Copyright Office (Library of Congress, Washington, D.C. 20559) requesting their free circular No. R22 entitled "Searches," which deals with the problem of determining whether a work is copyrighted. If the book does turn out to be in the public domain, you could rewrite these historical accounts, bringing the language up-to-date. Then send queries to publishers especially interested in American history, as listed in WRITER'S MARKET.

Performance Is Not "Publication"

Q. *I intend to give oral nonprofit readings of poetry that is under contract for future book publication. Would such reading in any way endanger my future copyright? Is there any good, practical reason to first copyright such poetry as a lecture, then later change its category to book?*

A. Under the copyright law, your readings of poetry would not jeopardize your statutory copyright on your book—as long as you make sure no recordings are being made of your readings. If copies of such recordings were distributed with your authorization, these could jeopardize your future book copyright.

Poetry Book

Q. *In arranging to publish a volume of one's poems, what is the proper and simplest procedure for securing release of copyright from publishers of magazines where the poems first appeared? Must individual letters be written to each editor giving the titles and dates of publication of the various verses, or could I make a mimeographed form in sets of three and a very simple request note? Supposing a magazine has now ceased publication and possibly the original publisher or editor is deceased. Could I ignore a release request?*

A. The basic letter can be the same; all you'd have to do would be to change the poem titles and publication dates for each. So a mimeographed form would probably save you time. Even though the magazine is no longer being published, or the copyright owner is deceased, the copyright still continues to run the course of its term and would be owned either by the publisher or his heirs. The release request should *not* be ignored. You may have to write to the Copyright Office for the most recent address on its records for the copyright owner.

Fictional Dialog in a Biography?

Q. *In the writing of biographies for children, is it possible to make the reading more interesting through use of fictional dialog and setting? If so, to what extent can liberties be taken, in order to assure a relatively accurate account of the nonfictional material while providing "readability" for youngsters?*

A. Fictionalized biographies are frequently used for both adult and juvenile readers. Working with the basic facts, you may create conversations and incidents that will best dramatize them. But be careful not to devise anything that would not be in keeping with the character of the subject or his times.

Children's Plays

Q. *My problem concerns a children's play I have written in which some of the characters are dolls or cartoon characters that have been made into dolls. Do I have to obtain permission from these doll manufacturers and the cartoon originators before I can use them? If so, how? I would also appreciate any information you might give me concerning markets for children's plays.*

A. When in doubt, it is always safest to ask for permission. Write the doll manufacturers (any large toy shop could provide their names and addresses) and the cartoon originators in care of the movie studios or newspapers that present their work. Explain your project and request permission to use the characters' names in the way you have described. Be sure to enclose SASE. Some markets for children's plays are listed in WRITER'S MARKET under the play publishers, play producers, juvenile magazine and education trade journals sections.

Permission to Quote

Q. *If I want to include a remark (good or bad) in an article about a magazine or article I have read, or comment on something I saw on TV, am I free to do so or do I have to obtain permission from the writer? I'm not going to quote, but will mention actual names.*

A. You may make the comments you wish concerning actual names and places without getting permission of the people involved. Just make sure your statements are accurate and not libelous.

Will the Real JB Stand Up?

Q. *How careful must a fiction writer be with names he contrives but which could very well turn out to be the names of living persons? For example, if I name the villain in a story Jack Bowlton. Could a real Jack Bowlton appear and sue me for defamation of character for characterizing him as a villain? Also, what became of the old disclaimer which used to read something like "Any similarity to persons, etc., is strictly coincidental"?*

A. Unless the real Jack Bowlton happened to be circumstantially very similar in personality and actions to the fictional character you gave that name, there probably wouldn't be any cause for legal recourse. The old disclaimer probably doesn't appear any more because the person who can prove that a real person was used in a fictional account and can also prove defamation or invasion of privacy many still have legal recourse in spite of the disclaimer.

Religious Order

Q. *I am preparing to write a novel with a religious order as the background. All characters are fictional but I would like to use fact for places, rules of the order and other pertinent data. Is it necessary to get permission from the Superiors of this order?*

A. To gain the specific practical information you need, yes, it would be best to contact the Superiors of the order about which you will be writing.

Old Songs

Q. *I have read children's plays in which poems were sung to the tunes of old-fashioned songs. Where do the authors write to get permission to use such old airs as "Flow Gently Sweet Afton," "Jingle Bells," etc.?*

A. Anyone may use such music without getting permission because these songs are in the public domain. Well-known current songs and their copyright dates are indexed by title in the *Variety Music Cavalcade* available in large public libraries.

Reprint Rights?

Q. *As a newcomer to the writing profession, I find the procedure for reselling an article or story confusing. Having used* WRITER'S MARKET *as a guide, I find many publishers listed as buying first and second rights. Is this publisher purchasing the right to print an article twice? After a story has been sold once, does the term "second rights" apply to each consecutive sale? Do third and fourth rights apply or do reprint rights come into effect at that time? Also, if a publisher has a policy of purchasing first serial rights, must the author request, in writing, reprint rights, or is this simply a matter of courtesy? Much of my writing has been to small religious magazines. I have been told the possibilities of selling a story numerous times are good because of the nonconflicting circulations. Supposing a story has already sold three times, would I signify this by printing 'Reprint Rights' in the right-hand corner, followed by names of the three publishing companies and the dates purchased, or is this listing unnecessary?*

A. When a publisher buys first and second rights, it means he will consider material which either has not been published before or which has been previously published. Second rights means he buys (usually for a lower price) the right to publish again an article, story or poem that has already appeared in another noncompeting publication. If a publisher purchases first serial rights, the author must request permission from the original publisher for transfer of other rights back to him. In the upper right-hand corner of your manuscript, type "reprint rights offered" and then perhaps as a last page to the manuscript, list places where the story has previously appeared or been purchased.

Watch the Check Too!

Q. *If I sell a novelette to any publisher, and some movie producer reads it in the magazine and wants to buy the movie rights, does he* *buy from me or the publisher? Must I reserve some kind of rights? Would the publisher be entitled to part of the money paid for the movie rights?*

A. Reserving movie rights to a novelette depends on what rights you sell to the magazine in which it initially appears. Most magazines buy only "first serial rights." Some magazines, however, buy "all rights," which would give them complete return of money on any subsidiary sale of the story to movies, TV, etc. If you want to reserve these other rights to yourself, when you submit your novelette to a magazine publisher, you must type in the upper right-hand corner "First North American Serial Rights Only." The magazine editor will know these are the only rights you care to sell. You should, however, also notice any check from the magazine publisher, since sometimes the endorsement on the check indicates the magazine is buying all rights. Often the accounting department of a magazine does not know what your manuscript indicated and if their normal procedure would be to buy all rights, the check will so indicate. By endorsing the check, you would be thereby giving away the rest of the rights, even though your manuscript had indicated you were interested in selling first rights only.

Resell?

Q. *I do not understand the system of "rights." Does this mean that if I sell a story to one magazine that I could resell the same story to another magazine?*

A. Many different rights (serial, book, TV, etc.), are involved in literary property. If you sold only first serial rights, for example, you could resell a story of yours that had previously appeared in another magazine.

Stole Your Story?

Q. *In a recent issue of a magazine appeared an article on the medical profession that was strikingly similar to an essay I had written* *three years before, even to the title. The general theme of the essay was the appalling lack of sympathy on the part of doctors today, even down to specific allusions, similes and general wording. I know that my essay was seen by several people in the "literary" world, and I'm naturally suspicious. I am really upset to think that I am forced to forget about submitting my piece anywhere else because they are so similar.*

A. It is one of the frustrating facts of the freelance writer's life to find that an idea he has, someone else has had also and beaten him to publication with it—sometimes even using the same words. You're not forced to forget about submitting your manuscript elsewhere. Many articles are published on the same subject in a vareity of publications within a two- or three-year period. If your article is well written, and hits the right magazine at the right time, publication of the other article will not be a deterrent to publication of yours.

Who Owns What?

Q. *Suppose Smith wrote a manuscript, in first draft, and gave it to Jones to read? Jones, a professional writer, keeps the manuscript, and in due time writes a book based on Smith's manuscript. If the book sells, and/or a movie is made from it, or paperbacks are published, or any other form of benefit derives from the sale of this book, does Smith have any rights in this book or the benefits therefrom?*

A. Much would depend on the agreement Smith made with Jones when he gave him his manuscript. Why, for instance, did Smith allow Jones to keep the manuscript? Smith might be able to take this matter to court as an infringement of his copyright, which protected his unpublished manuscript. In doing so, though, he'd have to prove that Jones actually copied his exact language or the development, treatment, arrangement or sequence of ideas in the work. And he would have to take legal action within the period of the applicable statute of limitations. It would, of course, be more desirable if Smith and Jones could work out some financial arrangement agreeable to both, rather than go to the expense of court action.

Translation Rights

Q. *A few months ago, while in Vienna, I read in an Austrian magazine a short article that I found impressive. I asked the doctor-author for the translation rights into English which he gladly gave me. Under whose name should one ask for the copyright — in the name of the author or translator?*

A. Publishers of periodicals usually copyright all articles, and then, upon request, assign the copyright to the author. In the case of a translation, the assignment of copyright will depend on the deal made between the owner of the basic copyright and the translator. You will have to settle this question with the doctor who granted you translation rights. (Incidentally, you had best also make sure the doctor *had* the rights to give you. Query the Austrian magazine to verify that he had the translation rights.)

Book Rights to Stories

Q. *Does a writer retain subsequent rights to his own stories published in a magazine? I have had seven confession stories purchased and printed by one company. Now I want to market these pieces as a collection in one book. Do I need permission from the original publisher? Suppose I rewrite these stories and have them registered as a book manuscript with the Copyright Office? Would I then be able to offer it for sale?*

A. You will have to check with the publisher who purchased your confession stories to determine who owns the copyright, book rights, etc. To register the rewritten stories with the Copyright Office in book form, the book must be published (printed) and carry the copyright notice.

Movie and TV Rights

Q. *How does an author keep movie and TV rights when a book is published?*

A. Read, very carefully, the clause in your book contract that pertains to those rights. The Authors Guild recommends that book contracts should give the author 90% and the publisher ten percent of movie and TV sales. Read the contract carefully before signing it.

41. Copyright

Copyright

Q. *How important is it for a new writer, or any writer for that matter, to secure a copyright for his book manuscript before submitting it to trade houses? Isn't it safe to entrust this somewhat bothersome detail to the publisher when and if publication is insured?*

A. The publisher who buys the manuscript usually copyrights the book in your name. The publisher's contract usually discusses the copyright procedure.

Copyrighting a Book

Q. *What is the approximate cost to copyright a book?*

A. The fee for registering a copyright claim is ten dollars. Make your check or money order payable to the Register of Copyrights, Copyright Office, Library of Congress, Washington, D.C. 20559.

Getting Permission

Q. *I would like to use some material in a book for my own research. Even though the copyright date is as recent as 1950, the publisher is no longer in business and the author is deceased. The book was copyrighted by the publishing house. Does the book and all its* *contents now revert to public domain? If not, how do I get permission to use the material?*

A. Even though the publisher is not currently in business, he still owns the copyright, which has to run its course of 28 years under the old copyright law. You would need his permission to use the material. Contact the Copyright Office in Washington, D.C. for the most recent address on its records for the publisher. Also, check with the local Chamber of Commerce of the city in which the publisher was located.

Magazines Copyrighted?

Q. *How does a writer know which magazines are not copyrighted? Is there a way I can state on my poems, fillers and manuscripts that I want my work copyrighted? How can an author obtain a separate copyright?*

A. Before you submit a manuscript to a magazine, you should ascertain whether that magazine is copyrighted. Look for the copyright notice which usually appears at the bottom of the Table of Contents page. To copyright your material that may appear in an uncopyrighted publication, write to the Copyright Office for an Application for Copyright for a "contribution to a periodical." At the bottom left-hand corner of your manuscript's first page, type your own copyright notice: © Your Name, date. As soon as the work is published with your copyright notice and made available to the public, register your claim by mailing to the Copyright Office the application form plus two complete copies of the publication containing your work, and the registration fee of ten dollars.

Copyright Symbol

Q. *When submitting a manuscript, should the writer place the symbol © "copyright by ... author's name, all rights reserved" on the manuscript copy? Or is this unnecessary? What is the procedure regarding copyright when submitting a manuscript?*

A. Most magazines copyright the entire contents of their publication, which covers your individual contribution, so it's not necessary to include the copyright line when submitting to a copyrighted publication. If you're submitting to an uncopyrighted publication, however, follow the procedure in the previous answer.

English Translation

Q. *I want to write a story in which I would use three verses from* The Rubaiyat of Omar Khayyam. *Are his verses, rendered into English by Edward Fitzgerald, in the public domain?*

A. Whether the English translation of *The Rubaiyat* that you have, which was copyrighted originally in 1938, has been renewed should be investigated before using that particular English version. A letter to the Register of Copyrights, Library of Congress, Washington, D.C., could probably determine whether that copyright is still in effect.

Copyright Expiration

Q. *A book passes into public domain after a certain number of years. Should these years be counted from the original publication date or from the date of the last reprint to determine if the book is still under copyright?*

A. Under the former copyright law, a copyright could be taken out on a book for 28 years and renewed once for another 28 years. (Since 1962, copyright expirations were renewed year by year through 1977 while the new copyright bill was under consideration by Congress.) If the copyright is renewed on a book, subsequent editions will show the new copyright date on the flyleaf. If there is any question about whether a subsequent edition of a book has a renewed copyright, see the *Catalog of Copyright Entries,* at your library, which lists books that have been copyrighted.

Humor Collection

Q. *For the last 15 years I have been collecting jokes, riddles, funny sign slogans and humorous writings. I've gathered these from friends, acquaintances, therapists, etc. I don't have a clue as to their origins, and I don't know if they are copyrighted or in the public domain. My problem is this: I am attempting to write a book (probably paperback length, incorporating the idea that a little humor in one's life will make the rough road of rehabilitation a little easier). But since I can't identify the author of some of these masterpieces-of-humor, how can I protect myself against possible plagiarism suits?*

A. Short gags and jokes cannot be copyrighted, so you wouldn't have any difficulty in assembling those in a book. Two-hundred to 300-word short prose humor pieces, however, might present a problem. If they did appear originally in copyrighted publications, you would have to rewrite them substantially to avoid possible suit for plagiarism.

Book on Copyright

Q. *I'm a young writer with work I'd like to send to magazines, but I don't understand about copyrights. I'd like to know the name of a good book explaining copyrights in layman terms.*

A. The new Copyright Law and its ramifications for writers are detailed in *Law and the Writer,* edited by Kirk Polking and Leonard S. Meranus (Writer's Digest Books.)

Copyright Unknown

Q. *Does it cost anything to have the Copyright Office check to see if a certain old book is still copyrighted?*

A. The Library of Congress has a search fee of ten dollars per hour to search for copyright. Most searches take at least an hour or two. For further information on the book in question, you might write the Register of Copyrights, Library of Congress, Washington, D.C. 20559.

Radio Material

Q. *What is the copyright status of radio broadcast material—helpful hints, short features, poetry, recipes, etc.? Can this material be re-used verbatim or are there restrictions?*

A. Radio scripts *can* be copyrighted, so your use of brief items should be governed by fair use guidelines. In considering fair use, decide: 1) whether use is for profit or nonprofit; 2) the nature of the copyrighted work; 3) how much you're using; 4) how it could affect the market value of the work you're quoting from. For an explanation of copyright and its application to radio and TV, see *Law & The Writer,* (Writer's Digest Books).

Newspaper Column

Q. *What copyright protection do I have on material used in my weekly newspaper column on sewing? A friend of mine would like me to use some of her ideas in my column, giving her credit. Would she receive any copyright protection?*

A. Unless the newspaper as a whole or your column in particular is copyrighted, there is no protection for the material. This applies to your friend's items as well as your own. If you want future columns copyrighted in your name, write for further information to the Copyright Office, Library of Congress, Washington, D.C. 20559.

Copyright Advertising Art?

Q. *Is advertising art and lettering in national magazines copyrighted? I plan to use text, photos and drawings from parts of different ads and combine them in a paste-up to be photographed and printed as an original work.*

A. Such work is copyrightable, so you'd better get permission before you start cutting and pasting.

Submitting Maps

Q. *I am preparing a travel article for which I will need maps as part of the illustrations. I don't know what kind of map to submit. Do I need permission to reproduce maps?*

A. Maps are copyrightable, so permission would be necessary to reproduce a previously published, copyrighted one. Submit the map you think best for your article along with copyright owner's address so that the editor can write for reprint permission if he decides to use it.

Copyright Law

Q. *I would like any information I can get regarding the copyright law on books.*

A. The copyright law is this: A book may be copyrighted for a period of the author's life plus 50 years. Also write to WRITER'S DIGEST, enclosing a SASE, for a free copy of the reprint, "Copyright: The Clauses of '78."

News Story

Q. *Occasionally I see a "hot" news story in a newspaper with a copyright. Can you give me a general idea about when such a copyright is advisable? Does a poor man's copyright (sending a copy of the article to yourself through the mails) suffice? It is my understanding that anything appearing in a newspaper becomes public domain after 24 hours. If that is correct, does it also apply to Sunday supplements?*

A. If you think your "hot" news story has reprint value to you in a subsequent book of your own, or someone else's anthology, that might be reason to take out your own copyright. No, sending a copy of the article to yourself through the mails won't give you copyright protection. Instead, write the Copyright Office for an application form for a "Contribution to a Periodical." Anything appearing in an *un*copyrighted newspaper or Sunday supplement immediately—not 24 hours later—falls into public domain on publication.

Fair Use?

Q. *If I lift paragraphs or short portions from published, copyrighted sources and duplicate and sell these for a profit, would that be a violation of copyright laws? And if so, would the publisher be likely to give me permission without fee to use his materials if I submitted a written request? If there was a fee, about how much would it be? I am making final arrangements to start a service in the field of religion, which consists of short-length abstracts, extracts, quotations, mini-bibliographies and how-to-do-it ideas taken from other published sources.*

A. As long as your're crediting the source and picking up only "short-length" copy, it probably would come under the fair use provision of the copyright law. A rule of thumb in deciding how much copy you can use without prior permission from a copyrighted publication is this: "Am I impairing the fair market value of the original by the amount of copy I'm using?"

Poetry in a Book

Q. *I've had poetry published in magazines such as* Jack and Jill *and* Humpty Dumpty's Magazine, *and as a beginning writer in this field I have several questions. Both magazines buy "all rights." If, in the future, I want to submit poems that have appeared in these magazines to a book publisher, how do I go about getting permission to do so? Also, if poems are accepted by a magazine that buys only "first North American serial rights," must I also get permission from them? Is there any charge for getting permission to use poems already published?*

A. Write the original publishers to see if you can get all but first serial rights released to you for the purpose you mention. They may not release the rights to you, but they may grant permission to a book publisher to use them as long as the magazine's original copyright line appears on the acknowledgment page. Write the publisher as soon as your work is published and ask the editor to return all other rights to the poems to you—which they'll do, if they bought only first rights. Some magazine publishers who bought all rights will expect you or the book publisher to pay a permissions fee. Those who bought only first rights may or may not expect a permissions fee.

Reassign Rights

Q. *Can rights be reassigned to me from a magazine that is now defunct?*

A. If the magazine was owned and published by a still-operating corporation or association, the author's material would still be their property. You might contact the rights and permissions department of the organization that published the now-defunct magazine. If you can't locate any present owners, then indicate that fact to the editor to whom you're trying to sell reprint rights.

Selling to Uncopyrighted Magazines

Q. *How can I protect my rights to an article if I sell it to an uncopyrighted publication? Is there a way I can copyright it myself?*

A. The only way you can protect your rights in an uncopyrighted magazine is to take out a special copyright on your article alone and see that the correct copyright notice and your name appear on the first page of the article in the magazine in which it's published. Send two copies of the printed article with a copyright notice and completed application form plus ten dollars to the Copyright Office, Library of Congress, Washington, D.C. 20559. You must follow this procedure for each article you sell to an uncopyrighted magazine if you want to keep your material from falling into the public domain.

Comic Strip Copyright?

Q. *I have created a comic strip from a number of cartoon characters that I have invented. This effort was actually quite unintentional and came from idle moments of doodling on paper. I believe these comics would have a great deal of public appeal. My goal is to have them published as a daily newspaper feature. Any help you can give me concerning the following questions would be most appreciated: How is a comic strip copyrighted? How does a syndicate operate? What part do they play in publishing comics? How does one get his work syndicated?*

A. Write the Copyright Office, Library of Congress, Washington, D.C. 20559 for information about copyrighting comic strips. Getting started in comic strip publication might best be done on a local level —that is, by approaching newspapers in your own and surrounding towns. Local or regional acceptance would enhance your chance of having the strip syndicated. Syndicates make their sales to publishers on a commission basis. They need samples of material proposed for syndication, so they can reach a decision about the material and the creator's ability to sustain a steady stream of production. All submissions of this nature and all inquiries to syndicates must be accompanied by SASE large enough to handle the return of the material if it is found unacceptable. But since most syndicates prefer to be queried first, it might be wise to send a query letter before submitting samples for syndication review. For additional information, see *Artist's Market* (Writer's Digest Books).

42. Miscellaneous Questions

Increase Byline?

Q. *How can I increase the frequency of my byline while I am writing a nonfiction book?*

A. That's a tough one, unless there are two of you. It's difficult to write XXX hours a day finishing the book manuscript while at the same time writing articles for other markets. If you feel the necessity to establish a known byline, you might not be doing the right thing by working on a nonfiction book first. Unless you have some special expertise in the subject matter of the book, it's tough to write (and market) a book. A few sales to magazines might be a better way to get established in the field before venturing into books. It's not impossible to sell a book if you are an unknown writer—but it is more difficult without previous background.

Ownership of Letters

Q. *I'm writing a book, and half of my research is done by writing letters. The interchange of thoughts and ideas between people has developed into an interesting aspect of the work. Is it absolutely necessary to get permission to reprint personal letters? Letters are from universities and hospitals, members of certain associations, and state representatives, among others.*

A. Yes, the thoughts, ideas, etc., in personal letters are the property of the *sender,* not the receiver, and you must get permission for their publication. Even though personal letters may seem to belong to the person to whom they are sent, to publish the letters, it is imperative to seek the letter-writer's permission in all cases.

Talent or Therapy?

Q. *I write in times of extreme despair, sorrow or stress. Might this be some indication of writing ability, or is this merely a form of comfort or therapy instead of alcohol, ungovernable temper, over-eating or other?*

A. A need to write does not necessarily denote an indication of ability or talent. It is not the motivation but the end result that counts. The channeling of tortured emotions into acts of creativity has sometimes been responsible for great works, such as the paintings of Van Gogh and the poetry of Keats.

Style

Q. *Can you please tell me why some magazines appear to have been written by the same author? The articles are in exactly the same style as the fiction. Can any of these magazines that seem to be written by one person be considered freelance markets?*

A. The stories and articles in certain magazines may seem to be the product of one prolific writer, but you can rest assured that they're usually not. What happens is that each magazine has a certain style peculiar to itself. In the hope of selling to this market, many writers are careful to slant to the known preferences at that market. Then, of course, editors may do some rewriting where material warrants it, and this too would tend to give an additional familiar touch to the work. These magazines are considered freelance markets.

Role Playing

Q. *I have often wondered whether a man can write effectively about a woman, or vice versa. If he is writing from the viewpoint of the woman or girl, could he possibly portray her problem and her various reactions to situations? Would he be better advised to choose a man as protagonist, or does it matter? What is the practice among successful writers?*

A. There is enough proof in the literature of the world that a writer can successfully portray a member of the opposite sex. Look at what Shakespeare did with Cleopatra, what Flaubert did with Madame Bovary, and don't forget what Margaret Mitchell did with Rhett Butler, to name just a few. The ease with which a male writer can slip into the consciousness of a female character and vice versa depends ultimately on the individual writer and how much insight he has into the workings of human nature, regardless of sex.

Write? Don't??

Q. *In an issue of* WRITER'S DIGEST, *one famous writer's advice to young writers was: "Don't write." In the same issue, another writer said, "To be a writer you must write." What's your reaction?*

A. These two statements, taken out of context, are not as contradictory as they may appear. Instead of spending all his time writing, the young writer should expose himself to experience, involving himself in life so that he will, in time, have something to write about. On the other hand, the writer should discipline himself in order to avoid all those little excuses he invents to put off sitting down and writing, i.e., sharpening pencils, changing typewriter ribbons, etc. The assumption is, of course, that he has something to say and just needs to make himself get started.

Dictating a Novel

Q. *Since I am going to tape record the second draft of a novel, I would appreciate your informing me about (1) the fastest talking* *pace with which I can expect a good typist to get everything down on paper, and later, to proofread the tape; (2) the exact wording to indicate punctuation, parentheses, italics, use of white spacing, etc.*

A. Record at your own pace. The typist will adjust her speed accordingly. A good typist should be able to punctuate correctly from the way in which the lines are spoken. You will, however, have to indicate parentheses by saying, "Open parentheses" ... and later, "Close parentheses." Say "Underline" when you want italics, and say "Paragraph" when you want to start a new paragraph. Before you begin, you can explain that you want double-spacing except where you indicate otherwise.

Writers' Conference

Q. *Do you know of any writers' conferences in the United States during November?*

A. Sorry, no. Most conferences are in the summer months, but for future reference, each year WRITER'S DIGEST's May issue contains a list of writer's conferences for that year.

A Writing Career

Q. *Do you help new writers get their start in the business world? I want to have a career in writing but I find it difficult to get started.*

A. A helpful booklet called *Jobs and Opportunities for Writers* has been published by WRITER'S DIGEST detailing the educational background, personality traits, and other requirements necessary for persons seeking certain types of staff writing jobs. The booklet also describes the average salaries paid and other details on each job.

Writers' Colonies

Q. *I have read so much about the days in Paris when writers gathered at certain addresses. Are there such places, where writers are* *known to collect informally today ... Paris, London, New York City, Chicago, or other cities in the world? How can I find out the streets or addresses of such places?*

A. No, there aren't any places in Paris, London, New York, Chicago or other major cities where writers are known to consistently gather, the way they did at the Ritz Bar in Paris and in certain cafes on the Left Bank. The MacDowell Colony in Peterborough, New Hampshire often has a few writers temporarily in residence along with artists and musicians, and occasionally on certain university campuses during writers' conferences several will happen to appear at the same time, but this is coincidental.

Pays on Publication

Q. *When a story is accepted with "payment on publication" is payment to the writer assured?*

A. Payment on publication is risky, though it is sometimes necessary to the beginning writer trying to get established. No, there is never a guarantee that an article will be published or paid for when it's accepted by the "pays on publication" market. Sometimes an article is accepted, with payment promised on publication, but editors change their minds and the piece is eventually returned to the author neither used nor paid for. Most publications, though they may take a long time to actually publish the piece, will pay after publication. It doesn't happen too often that you don't get paid, so it's worth the risk, if you want to get published. In the case of new markets that pay on publication, you have the risk that they may fold (discontinue publication) after one or two issues are published, and you'll never be paid. If a magazine folds, you will not be paid. You are, of course, free to submit that material to other markets.

Writers' "Average" Income

Q. *Every so often I see something about the average salary of the writer in America. But just who is this writer? The income men-*

tioned is so low that I cannot see how the supposedly high-priced TV and movie writers can be included in this average. Is the average writer someone like me who works fulltime at another job and has never sold anything for more than $15?

A. The "average salary" is presumably arrived at by a study of the incomes of all types of writers. Since there are so many more part-time and low-earning writers (like yourself) than there are top TV and screen writers, it is not hard to see why the resultant average income is not very high.

TV Commercials

Q. *Where can I send material for use in commercials? Is there a directory listing names and addresses of advertisers that might be potential markets?*

A. Very few advertising agencies will buy material for commercials from freelancers. You might try breaking into the business by approaching advertisers in your area. Ask for an appointment with the creative director. If you want to try national agencies in spite of this, look up the manufacturer in the *Standard Directory of Advertising Agencies,* available at large libraries.

Appendix:

Proofreading Symbols

Symbol	Meaning	Symbol	Meaning
ℓ	Take out	?/	Insert question mark
stet	Let it stand	!/	Insert exclamation
#	Insert space	(/)	Insert parenthesis
⊂	Close up entirely	[/]	Insert brackets
tr	Transpose	*lc*	Lower case
SC or ≈	Small capitals	¶	Paragraph
c & SC or ≡	Caps and small caps	⊏	Move left
caps or ≡	Capitals	⊐	Move right
V	Insert apostrophe	*Ital.* or —	Italic
⊙	Period	*bf*	Bold face
,/	Comma	⊓	Move up
:/	Colon	⊔	Move down
;/	Semicolon	*no* ¶	No paragraph
V V	Quotation marks	*ℓ#*	Take out space
=/	Insert hyphen		

Example

¶ — Posters, billboards, highway signs, newspaper and magazine headlines and advertising and the optometrist's eye examination charts are usully done in sans serif or square serif letters.

Sans serif includes two widely different types of letters. Gothic, as most commonly seen in newspaper headlines, is the older variety of sans serif. In the past twenty years or so many "new" sans serif faces have come into wide usage ⊙

Index

Books of Interest From Writer's Digest

The Beginning Writer's Answer Book, edited by Kirk Polking, Jean Chimsky, and Rose Adkins. "What is a query letter?" "If I use a pen name, how can I cash the check?" These are among 567 questions most frequently asked by beginning writers — and expertly answered in this down-to-earth handbook. Cross-indexed. 270 pp. $8.95.

Bylines & Babies, by Elaine Fantle Shimberg. The art of being a successful housewife/writer. 256 pp. $10.95.

The Cartoonist's and Gag Writer's Handbook, by Jack Markow. Longtime cartoonist with thousands of sales, reveals the secrets of successful cartooning — step by step. Richly illustrated. 157 pp. $9.95.

A Complete Guide to Marketing Magazine Articles, by Duane Newcomb. "Anyone who can write a clear sentence can learn to write and sell articles on a consistent basis," says Newcomb (who has published well over 3,000 articles). Here's how. 248 pp. $7.95.

The Confession Writer's Handbook, by Florence K. Palmer. A stylish and informative guide to getting started and getting ahead in the confessions. How to start a confession and carry it through. How to take an insignificant event and make it significant. 171 pp. $7.95.

The Craft of Interviewing, by John Brady. Everything you always wanted to know about asking questions, but were afraid to ask — from an experienced interviewer and editor of *Writer's Digest.* The most comprehensive guide to interviewing on the market. 244 pp. $9.95.

The Creative Writer, edited by Aron Mathieu. This book opens the door to the real world of publishing. Inspiration, techniques, and ideas, plus inside tips from Maugham, Caldwell, Purdy, others. 416 pp. $8.95.

The Greeting Card Writer's Handbook, by H. Joseph Chadwick. A former greeting card editor tells you what editors look for in inspirational verse . . . how to write humor . . . what to write about for conventional, studio and juvenile cards. Extra: a renewable list of greeting card markets. Will be greeted by any freelancer. 268 pp. $8.95.

A Guide to Writing History, by Doris Ricker Marston. How to track down Big Foot — or your family Civil War letters, or your hometown's last century — for publication and profit. A timely handbook for history buffs and writers. 258 pp. $8.50.

Handbook of Short Story Writing, edited by Frank A. Dickson and Sandra Smythe. You provide the pencil, paper, and sweat — and this book will provide the expert guidance. Features include James Hilton on creating a lovable character; R. V. Cassill on plotting a short story. 238 pp. $8.95.

Law and the Writer, edited by Kirk Polking and Leonard S. Meranus. Don't let legal hassles slow down your progress as a writer. Now you can find good counsel on libel, invasion of privacy, fair use, plagiarism, taxes, contracts, social security, and more — all in one volume. 249 pp. $9.95.

Magazine Writing: The Inside Angle, by Art Spikol. Successful editor and writer reveals inside secrets of getting your mss. published. 288 pp. $10.95.

Magazine Writing Today, by Jerome E. Kelley. If you sometimes feel like a mouse in a maze of magazines, with a fat manuscript check at the end of the line, don't fret. Kelley tells you how to get a piece of the action. Covers ideas, research, interviewing, organization, the writing process, and ways to get photos. Plus advice on getting started. 220 pp. $9.95.

Mystery Writer's Handbook, by the Mystery Writers of America. A howtheydunit to the whodunit, newly written and revised by members of the Mystery Writers of America. Includes the four elements essential to the classic mystery. A comprehensive handbook that takes the mystery out of mystery writing. 273 pp. $8.95.

1001 Article Ideas, by Frank A. Dickson. A compendium of ideas plus formulas to generate more of your own! 256 pp. $10.95.

Writing for Regional Publications, by Brian Vachon. How to write for this growing market. 256 pp. $10.95.

One Way to Write Your Novel, by Dick Perry. For Perry, a novel is 200 pages. Or, two pages a day for 100 days. You can start and finish your novel, with the help of this step-by-step guide taking you from blank sheet to polished page. 138 pp. $8.95.

Photographer's Market, edited by Melissa Milar. Contains what you need to know to be a successful freelance photographer. Names, addresses, photo requirements, and payment rates for 3,000 markets. 672 pp. $12.95.

The Poet and the Poem, by Judson Jerome. A rare journey into the night of the poem — the mechanics, the mystery, the craft and sullen art. Written by the most widely read authority on poetry in America, and a major contemporary poet in his own right. 400 pp. $9.95.

Sell Copy, by Webster Kuswa. Tells the secrets of successful business writing. How to write it. How to sell it. How to buy it. 288 pp. $10.95.

Songwriter's Market, edited by William Brohaugh. Lists 1,500 places where you can sell your songs. Included are the people and companies who work daily with songwriters and musicians. Features names and addresses, pay rates and other valuable information you need to sell your work. 480 pp. $10.95.

Stalking the Feature Story, by William Ruehlmann. Besides a nose for news, the newspaper feature writer needs an ear for dialog and an eye for detail. He must also be adept at handling off-the-record remarks, organization, grammar, and the investigative story. Here's the "scoop" on newspaper feature writing. 314 pp. $9.95.

Successful Outdoor Writing, by Jack Samson. Longtime editor of *Field & Stream* covers this market in depth. Illustrated. 288 pp. $11.95.

A Treasury of Tips for Writers, edited by Marvin Weisbord. Everything from Vance Packard's system of organizing notes to tips on how to get research done free, by 86 magazine writers. 174 pp. $7.95.

Writer's Digest. The world's leading magazine for writers. Monthly issues include timely interviews, columns, tips to keep writers informed on where and how to sell their work. One year subscription, $15.

The Writer's Digest Diary. Plan your year in it, note appointments, log manuscript sales, be prepared for the IRS. With advice such as the reminder on March 21 to "plan your Christmas story today." It will become a permanent annual record of writing activity. Durable cloth cover. 144 pp. $8.95.

Writer's Market, edited by William Brohaugh. The freelancer's bible, containing 4,500 places to sell what you write. Includes the name, address and phone number of the buyer, a description of material wanted and rates of payment. 960 pp. $14.95.

The Writer's Resource Guide, edited by William Brohaugh. Over 2,000 research sources for information on anything you write about. 488 pp. $11.95.

Writer's Yearbook, edited by John Brady. This large annual magazine contains how-to articles, interviews and special features, along with analyses of 500 major markets for writers. 128 pp. $2.50.

Writing and Selling Non-Fiction, by Hayes B. Jacobs. Explores with style and know-how the book market, organization and research, finding new markets, interviewing, humor, agents, writer's fatigue and more. 317 pp. $9.95.

Writing and Selling Science Fiction, compiled by the Science Fiction Writers of America. A comprehensive handbook to an exciting but oft-misunderstood genre. Eleven articles by top-flight sf writers on markets, characters, dialog, "crazy" ideas, world-building, alien-building, money and more. 197 pp. $8.95.

Writing for Children and Teen-agers, by Lee Wyndham. Author of over 50 children's books shares her secrets for selling to this large, lucrative market. Features: the 12-point recipe for plotting, and the Ten Commandments for Writers. 253 pp. $9.95.

Writing Popular Fiction, by Dean R. Koontz. How to write mysteries, suspense, thrillers, science fiction, Gothic romances, adult fantasy, Westerns and erotica. Here's an inside guide to lively fiction, by a lively novelist. 232 pp. $8.95.

Writing the Novel: From Plot to Print, by Lawrence Block. Practical advice on how to write any kind of novel. 256 pp. $10.95.

(1-2 books, add $1.00 postage and handling; 3 or more, additional 25¢ each. Allow 30 days for delivery. Prices subject to change without notice.)

Writer's Digest Books, Dept. B, 9933 Alliance Road, Cincinnati, Ohio 45242